THE BLACK PANTHER
The True Story.

DAN SHAW

The copyright to this book is owned by the author. All rights reserved. No part of this publication may be reproduced, stored in a retrieval system, or transmitted in any form, electronic, photocopying, mechanical, recording or otherwise, without prior permission from the author.

This book uses UK spelling

Cover Photograph: Author's Collection

The Black Panther
**Is the fourth instalment of the 'True Crime' series
by Dan Shaw.**

'The Krays: Their Life & Crimes'

'The Great Train Robbery'

'The Real Bank Job'

Are both available on Amazon as eBook & paperback.

Paperback versions are also available via some booksellers.

Contents

One: Early Life   8

Two: The Phantom   13

Three: Armed & Dangerous   18

Four: A Close Encounter   25

Five: Hide & Seek & Death   30

Six: Lesley Whittle   40

Seven: Dragnet, Robberies & Arrest   90

Eight: Trial, Prison & Other Events   112

Nine: Further Reading   122

FOREWORD

It was one day during the early 1970's that I learned the village I was growing up in had its own brush with the Black Panther. I was at school at the time and gossip went around the playground that our sub-post office had been robbed in the early hours of the morning by the notorious criminal. When I returned home after school the robbery was the only topic of conversation on everyone's lips. The sub-postmaster and his wife (whom I both knew well and who were universally liked by everyone who had dealings with them), had been woken up in the small hours by a man standing at the end of their bed. The intruder was armed with a sawn-off shotgun and demanded that the keys to the safe be handed over. Thankfully, the postmaster and his wife (who I'm not going to name) complied and as a result survived their encounter with Britain's most wanted man. Although they escaped physically intact, the psychological effect the robbery had on them was so significant that it haunted them for the rest of their lives.

Within a relatively short period of time of the attack the couple left the post office and attempted to find some peace in retirement but, unfortunately, the incident was to haunt them for the rest of their days. Although I was only young, I vividly remember the effect that the Black

Panther had on these two lovely people.

It's easy for us all not to appreciate what victims of crime – especially crimes of a violent nature – suffer and very easy not to be able to comprehend the emotional scars which are left behind.

Criminals, if brought to justice, will only ever be sentenced to prison – in most circumstances they are guaranteed to be released. In contrast, their victims are condemned to a life sentence of mental torture.

Dan Shaw.

One: Early Life

Donald Neilson was born in Bradford, in the then West Riding of Yorkshire, England, on August 1st 1936. Life was hard for the working classes, with long working hours and the drudgery of the daily grind taking its toll on many of the city's inhabitants. Nielsen's father, Gilbert, worked in the textile industry and his mother, Phyllis, looked after the family home, the role which was the norm for women in those days.

Little is known about Nielson's formative years save for the fact that he was subjected to merciless teasing by virtue of the fact that the family name was Nappey. His surname was often shortened to nappy (for US readers, nappy is the name given to a diaper) and used as the basis for a plethora of torment.

When Nielson was just 10 years old his mother died from breast cancer, aged 33. With his father working and unable to look after the young Nielson, he was sent to live with his grandmother. Nielson's obvious unhappiness was compounded by these circumstances and, while never academically minded, his education suffered accordingly. Whenever possible Nielson make sure he didn't attend school.

It was during his adolescence that Nielson had his first brush with the law. He was arrested for shop breaking just a year after his mother's death, aged eleven, but instead of finding himself in front of the magistrates', he was given a police caution.

Aged 15, Nielson finally left school and began work in a succession of dead-end labouring jobs within the building industry. Uneducated and uninterested, at that point in time it would appear that Nielson's future work life would be confined to such low paid, menial employment. There was one thing however which would take him away from his environment and open up a whole new raft of possibilities for the young Nielson.

On August 1 1954, Neilson turned 18. This meant he was now eligible for call up for two years National Service. Since the end of world war two, some nine years previously, all young males were required to undertake compulsory military service. Neilson was no exception to this rule and shortly after his birthday his call up papers arrived. He reported for duty with the King's Own Yorkshire Light Infantry regiment at Pontefract barracks, Pontefract, near Wakefield, in the West Riding.

Unlike many among his fellow conscripts, Neilson took readily to army life. He adapted quickly to the discipline and rigours of training but ultimately failed the eight-week basic training course. At that particular point in time, it would appear that his ability to be taught was mirroring his experiences in school. However, and in direct contrast to his schooldays Neilson found himself blossoming within the military.

At that period in time the British army was heavily involved in peace keeping and counter insurgency operations across the empire. As a result the young Nielson (who was then still Donald Nappey) found himself in Kenya.

Since the end of the Second World War, the Kenyan African Union (KAU) had been campaigning for land reforms and political rights. There had been little significant movement on the part of the British during that time so the KAU began to take a more militant approach to their campaign. By 1952 the KAU were attacking political opponents, as well as raiding white owned farms. By October of that year the situation had deteriorated to the point where the British declared a state of emergency. Subsequently, military units were dispatched to the country in order to put down the rebellion and Neilson was one of the soldiers would travel to Kenya with the KOYLI.
After the deployment to Kenya, Neilson and his battalion were moved to Cyprus then Aden where more civil unrest was fermenting.

Aged just nineteen, Neilson married his twenty-year-old girlfriend, Irene Tate. The couple settled into military married life and, when his National Service was completed, Neilson harboured an ambition to sign on as a regular soldier. While it appears he would have been content to remain in the military, perhaps even for a full twenty-two years service, Irene was not as keen on the army life as her husband. She had been asking Neilson to leave the army for much of the time they had been married as soon as his National service came to an end so, in 1958, he finally conceded two her wishes and, instead of joining the regular army, he was demobbed.

The pair returned to Yorkshire and set up home in Bradford where Neilson resumed work in the building trade. With a wife to support and bills to pay, Neilson soon began to struggle. The money he was making as a lowly labourer could not be made to stretch far enough. In the hope of turning around his fortunes, Neilson decided to take the plunge into self-employment. He opened a carpenter's shop and set to work as a Joiner, working throughout the Bradford area and beyond. Though he had picked up some carpentry skills from this time working as a labourer, they were not enough to ensure he could make any real headway in the joinery trade. The frustration Neilson began to feel was compounded by the news that his wife was pregnant. Preparations for the arrival of his child saw Neilson begin to spend money he didn't have. He put a deposit down on a small terraced house into which he and Irene moved prior to her giving birth.

Soon after their daughter was born, Neilson

decided to change the family name by deed poll from Nappey to Neilson. This decision was taken for one reason only; to save his daughter from the same humiliation he had suffered at school. There are several theories as to where he discovered the new family surname; some say he had seen the name Neilson on the side of the local ice cream van. A more plausible explanation was the fact that he had brought a small taxi firm from a local man named Neilson. By acquiring the taxi firm, Neilson hoped to expand his income to the point where he could keep himself, his wife and baby daughter in a modicum of luxury.

Unfortunately, Neilson's lack of business acumen meant that his new acquisition began to struggle. He now had two businesses which were not only failing to perform in the manner he had hoped, but were teetering on the edge of collapse.

Neilson now knew that while his accomplishments in the building trade and taxi business would never realise the rewards he hoped for, he had a set of skills which – perhaps – could be adapted in order to turn his fortunes around. His time with the army in Kenya, Cyprus and Aden meant he could move through hostile environments without been seen and was able to properly plan military style manoeuvres. Neilson realised that if he could adapt what he had learned in the army then it was entirely possible that that he will be able to make a handsome living from crime....

Two: The Phantom

Donald Neilson took the plunge into a life of crime with a measure of planning and caution which were to be the watchwords of his new career. After some deliberation he decided that the best course of action would be to work as a housebreaker, burglarising domestic properties throughout the Bradford area. His targets, he decided early on, were to be homes found in the more affluent areas of the town. His wouldn't be random, opportunist, Crimes but carefully planned and carried out military style operations. If done correctly, Neilson knew that he will be able to carry out his work without fear of capture.

The most important part of the scheme was Neilson's determination that he would always work alone and would never speak about his exploits to anyone under any circumstances. His experience in the carpentry trade meant that Neilson was familiar with the construction of the various types of windows fitted into houses of that period. Unlike today, where almost all windows are of UPVC construction, in those days they were made from timber. There were also no anti-theft devices fitted and only simple stays or latches to secure them when open. Knowing how they were made and how they operated gave Neilson the advantage insofar as he was able to produce a simple yet effective method of breaching any type of window he encountered. Using a bit and brace and a short length of metal rod bent up at one end, Neilson could drill through the window frame at the required point before inserting the rod to disengage this day or latch inside, once done it would simply be a matter of sliding or pulling open the window before gaining entry to the property.

Being self employed game Neilson ample opportunity to both plan and execute his crimes. He devoted much of his working day to carrying out reconnaissance on the targets he had selected. Unlike the normal preconception of the burglar, who strikes during the hours of darkness, Neilson's priority was to hit properties when they were unoccupied, regardless of time of day. Leaving his car away from the scene he would approach on foot, using whatever route afforded the best cover. Once at the target property, Neilson would satisfy himself that it was indeed unoccupied before attempting to break in.

Neilson quickly began to rack up enough of a tally of victims among the usually crime free areas of Bradford to bring his activities to the attention of the borough police. Although the method of entry which Neilson had adopted was not unique to him, the fact that it was being used to attack homes within certain districts lead the police to believe they were dealing with just one perpetrator. The Criminal Investigation Department (CID) was soon put on the case and charged with bringing the culprit to justice as soon as possible. As the CID officers assigned to investigate this string of burglaries uncovered the pattern of offending and realised whoever was responsible was not the ordinary common or garden thief, but someone who took great care to cover his tracks. The nickname 'The Phantom' was attached to their quarry when the detectives realised he was managing to stay one step ahead of them.

Coincidentally, Neilson presumed the police would soon identify his method of operation and therefore come to the conclusion that they were looking for just one man. In an attempt to throw them off the scent, he made a conscious effort change his modus operandi at every available opportunity. However, and despite his best efforts, there was no way of disguising his preferred method of entry. Neilson decided that the only way to continue to evade the police was to widen his own area of operations.

In those days, there was little communication between neighbouring police forces. There were no computers and all intelligence relating to local Crimes and criminals were held in card index systems. While one force could request information on certain individuals and/or incidents from another, it was normally only ever done in circumstances where serious crimes had been committed. In the case of house burglary, there would be little reason for any police force to wish to search outside their own area.

Neilson appeared to derive some pleasure from the fact that he managed to go undetected, and the certain knowledge that his one man crime spree across the affluent suburbs of Bradford brought his activities to the attention of CID detectives will no doubt have been cause of further delight. That said, despite his best efforts, he was still not bringing in the amounts of money he thought he would via this particular criminal venture. Travelling to commit crimes soon became problematic, as it meant Neilson was forced to spend more time away from home and his businesses than he could account for, add to that the ongoing issue of inadequate hauls meant that he began to carry out more burglaries on his home turf.

Neilson always kept abreast of local news events and was aware that there appeared to be no overt police hunt for him, but his instinct told him that behind the scenes, somewhere at Bradford police headquarters, the CID would be quietly working away in an effort to identify 'The Phantom'.

***

Neilson's housebreaking spree continued and, despite its disappointing returns, he still ventured beyond Bradford into the greater West Riding and even neighbouring counties in the hope of hitting the burglary jackpot.

It was on one such trip – to rob a property in

Cheshire – that Neilson struck gold. In monetary terms the drive all the way from Bradford to Cheshire and back had hardly been worth the effort, however, there was on part of the haul which excited him. During the burglary, Neilson came across a gun cabinet into which he managed to gain entry. Inside he found several firearms, including shotguns, a rifle and a .22 calibre pistol. As well as the firearms there was quite a large amount of ammunition of various calibres to fit all these weapons. Neilson was delighted to come across the guns and enthusiastically emptied the cabinet of its contents.

Returning home to Bradford, Neilson was able to hide his stash of firearms. Although he wasn't sure of the use he intended to put them to, it was quite obvious that they would be invaluable at some stage in his quest to make big money from criminality….

THREE: Armed & Dangerous

By the start of the 1970's Neilson had committed approximately four hundred burglaries and, true to the nickname he didn't then know he'd been given by the police, he had indeed proved to be every inch a phantom. While he'd successfully managed to evade the police, the large paydays he so craved continued to evade him.

Neilson's enthusiasm for all things military had stayed with him since his National Service days and manifested itself in several unusual ways. He liked to wear combat fatigues and go on 'manoeuvres' onto the moors outside Bradford. He would often insist that his wife and young daughter accompany him on these exercises and bought an old Hotchkiss 'jeep' to allow the trio to range deep into the wilds of the moors where ramblers simply couldn't go.

It's difficult to imagine what was going through Neilson's mind while was out on these schemes, let alone what Irene and the child made of it all.

Planning and preparation was a key component of these trips and this attention to detail was something which Neilson obviously enjoyed, after all, the scrupulous manner with which he executed his burglaries had ensured he remained free from arrest.

Neilson had constructed a 'planning/operations'

room in the loft of his terraced house and it was into this he would retreat to make all the preparations he deemed necessary before conducting one of his housebreaking expeditions. The entrance to the room was kept locked and no one was allowed inside, Neilson made sure the key was kept well hidden. Aside from the maps and other materials he used to plan his burglaries, the room was used as storage for the outfits he chores to wear while conducting his operations. In the main, Neilson would dress himself in military type fatigues, sometimes black in colour if he knew he would be breaking into a property during the hours of darkness.

The loft room had also become home to his cache of weapons. In keeping with his army training, Neilson was most fastidious in maintaining the guns he had stolen in one of his break-in's, making sure they were clean and functioning correctly at all times. Neilson spent many long hours in his loft hideaway, obsessing over maps, planning infiltration and ex filtration rules and considering contingency plans should he be compromised before, during or after one of his burglaries. It was here that he decided to change his pattern of criminal behaviour once and for all. Yes, he had been making a living from burglary but the simple fact remained that he could never achieve the rewards he so craved by breaking in to houses.

The move away from burglary was not a rash decision on Neilson's part; it was undertaken only after thorough appraisal and satisfying himself that he will be able to conduct this new venture with the same immunity from arrest which he had enjoyed over the past decade. From now on, Neilson decided, he was to retire from house breaking and begin a new criminal career as an armed robber.

***

Neilson went to great lengths when deciding the type of target he would concentrate on. The usual armed robbery would take place on a bank during business hours. The notion of holding up such a place in broad daylight, with all the possibilities of things going wrong which that entailed did not appeal to Neilson, and the more he thought about it the more convinced he became that it simply was not feasible. Neilson was a lone operator who relied on stealth to achieve his objectives, therefore the crash-bang immediacy of a bank robbery did not appeal to him. There must be, he thought, an alternative to banks, places which held large amounts of cash on the premises which he could the attack and where he could go undiscovered during and after the crime, at least long enough for him to make good his escape.

During those days, small sub-post offices abounded. Indeed, they were to be found in every village. Unlike banks with their sophisticated security systems, the small post offices were not particularly well protected from the attentions of armed robbers. There had been numerous instances of criminals walking into post offices brandishing firearms and demanding that the person behind the counter hand over cash. While this trend had been identified and steps taken to counter it, they were often rudimentary. The most sophisticated anti-theft measure was often a burglar alarm which could be initiated by pressing a panic button located somewhere beneath the counter. While it would sound an alarm, there will be no one within the immediate vicinity to interdict the robbers as they fled the scene, the criminals knew this and would simply ignore the ringing alarm bell and continue with their mission of robbing the post office of its money. Sometimes alarms were connected to the telephone line and, if triggered, would immediately alert the local police station of any incidents; however these particular systems were few and far between, often the common or garden sub-post office had nothing more than a telephone with which to alert the authorities in the event of a robbery taking place.

It was for these reasons that Neilson decided to concentrate his efforts on the small village sub-post office, that said, he knew he wouldn't go charging in during broad daylight waving a shotgun, with all the permutations for things to go wrong which that entailed; his particular brand of armed robbery would have a modus operandi all of its own.

Neilson was determined to capitalise upon the skills he had honed during his time as a burglar, making unseen approaches to his targets then entering surreptitiously before carrying out the robbery itself. In contrast to his house breaking, Neilson was now going to rely on the fact that he would encounter the occupants of the building. Sub-postmasters and their families would occupy purpose built accommodation above their workplaces. It was into these flats which Neilson planned to break. Once inside he would enter the main bedroom and wake the occupants, the sub-postmaster/mistress would then be ordered at gunpoint to either hand over the keys to the safe or be taken downstairs into the post office and made to open the safe themselves. Neilson would tie his victims up before a decanting the contents of the safe into a rucksack then leaving the scene.

He envisioned each raid to be a short and brutal affair. While his principal aim remained to steal money from the safe, Neilson knew he would deal with interference from the people he encountered with whatever level of violence he thought appropriate, including opening fire. His overriding priority was to evade capture at all costs and if this meant shooting someone, then so be it.

Neilson set to work preparing for his first robbery. He already had the appropriate clothing for the task, all black, including gloves and balaclava, as well as a sturdy pair of boots. He had taken one of the stolen double-barrelled twelve bore shotguns and cut down the barrels and butt to form a compact weapon which could be easily concealed and brought to bear in confined spaces. He was aware that he could not rely on a firearm alone. To this end, Neilson was determined to bring into play the unarmed combat skills he had learned while serving as an infantry soldier. During his time in the army, Neilson had been a most enthusiastic participant in not only unarmed combat in its military application, but had enjoyed other disciplines such as wrestling. As such, he was confident of his ability to get into physical confrontations anyone he may come across during the course of his robberies and who may decide to offer resistance.

During the course of his planning, and before the first robbery took place, Neilson had a change of heart, deciding that – if at all possible – he would attempt to find the keys to the safes himself, without waking the occupants of a target premises. He reasoned that should he be able to open the safe covertly then he could be away with the contents and make good his escape long before the crime was discovered.

Neilson took his time during this planning phase, he knew he had no need to rush things and to do so would be to invite disaster. Everything had to be as perfect as possible in order to satisfy him before he made his move. Pondering the possibilities of what may happen, Neilson decided to make sure he would be able to shoot or fight his way out of any situation. As well as the sawn off shotgun, he decided that on each 'operation' he would take along the .22 pistol, a large hunting knife and a homemade garrotte. After much deliberation, Neilson drew up a shortlist of potential targets which he further reduced to a final selection of post offices upon which he would begin his reign of robberies....

Four: A Close Encounter

It was a cold winter's night, February 10th 1972. Leslie Richardson and his wife Hilda were asleep in bed. The Richardson's ran a small sub-post office in Haywood, Lancashire. They were aware that an unknown man had been burglarising post office premises and stealing money from safes while people slept but, because the crimes thus far had taken place mostly in Yorkshire, they had no reason to believe whoever was responsible would pay them a visit.

At about 3.30am, Hilda was stirred from her sleep by what she later described as a 'scratching noise', Hilda listened for a few seconds before deciding that the noise was nothing to worry about and certainly not enough of an issue to wake her husband. Thinking no more of it she decided to go back to sleep. Unbeknown to her, 'scratching noise' was actually Neilson attempting to open the safe downstairs in the post office. She also didn't know that Neilson had been in the bedroom while the pair of them slept and taken a set of keys which he found in Leslie's trousers. Unfortunately for Neilson, the keys weren't the ones he was looking for, and he was forced to return to the bedroom in search of the correct one. Although she had closed her eyes, Hilda had not gone back to sleep, something in the back of her mind was telling her that all was not well. Soon she heard more noise, this time only a few feet away inside the bedroom itself. Not daring to look, a terrified Hilda shook Leslie awake proclaiming that she thought there was a rat loose in the room. Waking with a jolt, Leslie immediately spotted a figure in the darkness. Without hesitation he leapt from the bed in order to get to grips with the intruder. Before the unknown man could properly react, Leslie was on him and a ferocious struggle ensued. While this was happening Leslie called on to Hilda to run, she jumped from the bed and ran into the adjoining room. Amidst the struggle beyond one man suddenly produced a sawn-off shotgun from about his person and, in an obviously fake West Indian accent, he warned Leslie that the gun was loaded. Undeterred by the threat Leslie grabbed at the weapon and managed to get his fingers on the triggers. By this time the gun was pointing towards the ceiling and Leslie discharged both barrels harmlessly up into the ceiling and sending a shower of plaster down across the scene.

While this was happening, Hilda had reached the telephone. In the darkness and amid her panic, instead of dialling 999 to get the police she mistakenly dialled 000. When she finally realized her mistake she redialled and was put through to the police emergency response operator. Unfortunately, the sound of the shotgun being fired further scared the already terrified Hilda and all she said was "They're killing my husband!"

before dropping the receiver on to the cradle without telling the person on the other end of the line where she was calling from.

Hilda ran back out into the bedroom just as Leslie and Neilson were wrestling their way through the bedroom door and on to the landing. The fight continued down the stairs with neither man giving ground to the other. After trading a few blows, Leslie grabbed hold of Neilson for a second time. As Hilda look on Neilson attempted to counter Leslie's attack by kneeling him in the groin. It took several attempts by Neilson to force Leslie to let go and when he did he slumped to the ground in agony. Neilson took this as his cue to make his escape. Leaping over Leslie, Neilson ran for the kitchen and the open window through which he had gained entry into the property.

There was only one thing on Neilson's mind now and that was escape, he knew the post office had a telephone and he also assumed that, if she hadn't already, Hilda would be calling the police. Neilson knew he had to clear the area before the police could respond to the emergency call; time was short as even now patrol cars will be rushing to the scene.

Back at the scene, Leslie had recovered enough to instruct Hilda call the police a second time. When she got through she passed all the relevant information to the controller and was told that the police were on their way. Several patrol cars arrived at the scene only a few moments later, and once an initial description of the assailant was given them they in turn passed it on to other cars which were now cross graining the area in the hope of picking up whoever was responsible as they fled the scene. Unbeknown to the police they had narrowly missed Neilson as he had only just made it back to his car before the police search got into full swing.

During the scuffle Leslie had managed to remove Neilson's balaclava mask, thus exposing his face to both him and Hilda. The unknown intruder had left no incriminating evidence in his wake, so a possibility of his have been identified via Leslie and Hilda's description was the only real lead the police had to go on. An artist's impression was made and released to the press in the hope that someone, somewhere, may recognise the mystery man. However, it later transpired that the description given by Leslie and Hilda was inaccurate and the resulting impression bore no resemblance to Donald Neilson.

Back home in Bradford, Neilson took stock of events. He was aware that he had escaped by the narrowest of margins, indeed this incident had been the closest he came to capture. At that point Neilson vowed never to place himself in that situation again, from now on if he was challenged and that challenge threatened to spill over into physical confrontation, he would simply shoot first and not bother to ask question afterwards.

The prospect of committing murder did not bother Neilson, his overriding priority was money and being absolutely sure he was able to make a clean getaway each time he carried out a robbery.

Despite Neilson's best efforts to disguise his M.O, the police were quick to tie the failed Hayward robbery with the others which had happened at sub-post offices previously. Their investigation was ramped up because they were now no longer just looking for a burglar targeting sub-post offices, but a dangerous criminal who was carrying a loaded firearm and the obvious peril which his victims now faced. A call was sent out between various police forces across the north and midlands. They had a description of sorts, as well as an established pattern of offending so perhaps – just perhaps – someone might recognise a burglar whose modus operandi fitted that of the perpetrator or, better still, might just be able to put a name to the artist's impression?

Five: Hide & Seek & Death

Over the course of the next two years there was no let up in the activities of the mysterious post office robber; indeed it appeared that whoever was responsible had widened his sphere of operations to include targets further afield and he had made no more mistakes since his encounter with Leslie Richardson.

From the police's perspective the trail had gone cold, they were no closer to apprehending the suspect than they had been at the time of the Haywood robbery. Efforts to identify the mystery gunman by way of the media, or appealing to police forces nationwide had had drawn a blank. It was most frustrating indeed for the detectives to know they had a dangerous criminal at large and little prospect of affecting an arrest.

For his part, Neilson had not forgotten how close he had come to disaster that night in Haywood. Determined not to repeat what happened, he began to take even more precautions than usual with his preparation and planning; only executing his burglaries when he was sure the chances of success were firmly on his side. Now, before entering any target building, he would always cut the telephone lines. If he was compromised while on the premises, he reasoned that this would prevent the occupants from raising the alarm before he had chance to make his getaway. Neilson was always meticulous in his planning but now made it doubly sure during his reconnaissance of potential targets, that there were no dogs present. Neilson disliked dogs and was afraid of them so, as a result, he made sure that none of the post offices he intended to rob had a dog which could raise the alarm or attack him.

On February the 14th 1974, almost two years to the day since his encounter with Leslie Richardson, Neilson chose to rob another sub-post office.

Fifty-four year old Donald Skepper and his wife, Joanna, ran New Park Telegraph sub-post office on the outskirts of the quiet spa town of Harrogate, in the North Riding of Yorkshire. Geographically, it was only a short distance from Neilson's Bradford home and the twenty mile journey meant Neilson was confident he could be there and back without anyone knowing he'd left town. Neilson had selected the post office as a potential target some months previously and subsequently carried out his usual reconnaissance mission to find out the lay of the land. He was interested in the exact location of the target building and how it related to the surrounding area. Were there areas which would allow him to make an unseen approach? Could he park his car (which was stolen and fitted with false plates) somewhere where it wouldn't draw attention? If needs be, could he extricate himself from the scene before the police were able to respond?

Neilson's checklist had been satisfied and that night he set off to rob the post office. As usual he was armed with an assortment of weapons, including the sawn-off shotgun.

Arriving on the scene late, Neilson satisfied himself that all was quiet in and around the target building before setting to work drilling the window frame with his auger. After gaining entry to a downstairs room, Neilson picked his way through the darkness to the foot of the stairs. From here, he predicted, his crime would follow its usual pattern. He'd enter the main bedroom and, while the occupants slept, silently rifle through their belongings until he came across the key to the post office safe. He'd then retire downstairs and into the post office itself, open then empty the safe before vanishing into the night. The first thing the people upstairs would know about the incident was when they came into the post office the following morning and found the safe wide open.

As Neilson slowly ascended the stairs, placing his feet at the edges so as not to be caught out by squeaking boards, he listened intently for signs of life. His gun was at the ready and he knew what fate awaited anyone who dared to take him on.

Placing his hand on the doorknob, Neilson slowly opened the door just enough to allow himself to peek round it. Instead of finding a couple of people asleep, he was presented by a man and woman sat up in bed.

Donald and Joanna were every bit as shocked as Neilson, but Donald recovered almost immediately.

"Let's get him!" Donald exclaimed as he made to clamber out of bed. Suddenly, the sound of gunfire tore through the air, in the confines of the bedroom, the noise was magnified into even more ear-splitting proportions. Joanna saw Donald collapse back into bed, he was still sitting up but now slumped awkwardly. He'd been shot once, in the chest. A terrified Joanna attempted to comfort her husband.

"Oh my darling!" she cried as she watched Donald lapse into unconsciousness.

Meanwhile, Neilson was hurrying from the scene. He ran downstairs and scrambled through the window before fleeing towards where he'd parked his getaway car.

At Harrogate police station word was coming through that there'd been an incident at New Park post office. Details were sketchy, but initial reports indicated there may have been a shooting. Immediately, all available patrol cars were dispatched to the scene, blue-lighting their way to New Park from every direction. Despite the pandemonium which often accompanies such emergency calls, when information is unavailable to the responding officers and minutes can be lost establishing what has happened, the first units to arrive quickly realised the severity of the event and that it was most likely the work of the same man who had fought with Leslie Richardson. Calling in their suspicions over the radio set in motion another chain of events which were designed to catch the killer before he could escape.

Neilson had already made it back to his car by the time he heard the first sirens. The distinctive police 'two-tones' were cutting through the night, telling him that he had no time to lose. He threw his things into the boot (trunk) before slipping behind the wheel. He knew he had to resist the urge to drive away from the area at high speed because that act alone, if seen by one of the approaching police cars, would result in a chase and probable arrest. The best way to evade capture was to fight the impulse and drive as if he was on a Sunday outing.

Acting as rapidly as they were able, the police responded to the murder by setting up roadblocks and searching the area around the crime scene, but they were too late. Neilson had long gone, disappearing into the night back to Bradford.

The murder of Donald Skepper changed the game as far as both the hunters and hunted were concerned. From the police perspective, they were no longer dealing with an armed robber, but a man who was prepared to use lethal force without provocation. Ever since the incident with the Leslie Richardson the police had been expecting the worse, now, those fears were realised. It was imperative that the culprit was caught before he could strike, and kill, again.

As for Neilson, he knew he had been elevated to an absolute police priority. They would do everything possible to identify and arrest him.

The media interest in Donald's murder soon turned into a frenzy. Who was the killer and would the police catch him?

***

September 1974, some six months after the shooting at Harrogate, police lines of inquiry into the masked post office raider had dried up. Despite continuing media interest and the best efforts of detectives to push the investigation along, they were no closer to finding Donald Skepper's murderer. As far as the police were concerned history appeared to be repeating itself insofar as they had run into the same brick wall with the Hayward case.

On the 6th of the month, at the small sub-post office in Baxenden, near Accrington, Lancashire, post master Derek Astin and his wife Marion had retired to bed. Marion had already climbed in between the sheets but Derek was still sitting on the edge of the bed preparing to join her. Without warning, a man appeared in the doorway. He was dressed from head to toe in black and was wearing a ski mask type balaclava. In his hand was a pistol.

The intruder had no time to react as, without a second thought, Derek was up and onto him. The two men grappled and Derek managed to force his opponent into the bathroom. By this time Marion was out of bed and looking for something which could be used as an expedient weapon.

"Here! Hit him with this!" She shouted as she made to pass the only thing to hand – the vacuum cleaner – to her husband.

Two gunshots shattered the scene, they'd been fired in such quick succession that Marion thought there was only one. Derek slumped to the ground as the intruder pushed past her and ran away down the stairs. Marion was shocked to see skin and flesh spattered across the bathroom wall. Derek had been wounded in the shoulder and was bleeding profusely. Marion knelt beside him in a vain attempt to render first aid.

"Don't worry love, it's only your arm." Marion said, attempting to reassure him.

"It can't be." Derek replied before dying.

It was only then that Marion realised that Derek had also been shot in the back.

A couple of days later, during an interview with a local TV station, Marion spoke about her husband's killer. She pointed out the fact that he'd been dressed all in black and 'was as quick as a panther'. Picking up on this in his piece to camera, the reporter asked "where is the Black Panther?"

The media quickly adopted the name and the elusive killer was referred to by this title by everyone thereafter.

***

Less than two weeks later, on the 16th of September, the Black Panther struck again. This time his target was a sub-post office in Langley, in the Sandwell district of the West Midlands. Neilson was desperate for money and was determined to take what he could and apply whatever level of violence was required to do so. That same desperation, coupled with - perhaps - a realisation that the occupants of sub-post offices were now taking measures to protect themselves while sleeping and hide the keys to their safes where they couldn't be found meant that Neilson decided to ditch his normal method of operation in favour of a deliberately confrontational approach. This time there would be no brace and bit, Neilson knew how he would gain entry and what he would do when inside.

It was just after 6pm and, after closing the post office, Sidney Grayland and his wife, Margaret (who was sub-post mistress), had retired into the storeroom at the rear of the premises to do some stocktaking before finishing work for the evening. The sound of the back door being forced alerted them both to fact that someone was trying to break in. Sidney set off to confront whoever was responsible and had not gone far when a sudden explosion of gunfire shattered the silence. Sidney fell back, mortally wounded, onto the floor. Margaret found herself confronted by a man dressed in black, brandishing a handgun. The man demanded she hand over the key to the safe. A combination of shock, fear and defiance meant Margaret was unable or unwilling to comply. Without hesitation the intruder – who Margaret now recognised as the Black Panther – set about her with his fists. Margaret was subjected to a terrible beating before Neilson was finally able to get his hands on the keys. He left her in a heap, barely conscious, among the boxes and made his way into the post office where he opened the safe and stole £800 (£7,428 - $9,740 in 2022 values).

Margaret lay there semi-conscious and unable to move for three hours until she was discovered by a passing police constable. Unfortunately, Sidney had been dead for some time but Margaret was taken to hospital where she slowly recovered – at least physically recovered – from her injuries.

The attack on the defenceless Margaret Grayland reviled the nation and brought enormous pressure upon the police to catch the

Black Panther and end his reign of brutality.

Six: Lesley Whittle

With all the attention his activities were now attracting, Neilson decided to lay low for a while. He was confident that – despite their best efforts – the police still had nothing to go on and certainly no in inkling of the real identity of the Black Panther. Apart from a general description of his height and build (which was accurate) the police were still working with the artist's impression given them by Leslie and Neilson knew it bore no resemblance to him.

Just as he had been with his housebreaking exploits, Neilson was growing frustrated by the poor returns from his post office robberies. He realised that he could not go on indefinitely with his current enterprise. The odds of him being captured were shortening with each robbery, so Neilson decided to go for broke, committing one big job which would set him up financially for some years to come.

In his attic planning room, Neilson had been working out how to turn this ambition into reality. In fact he had been considering his proposal for three years, quietly studying his target and compiling all the information he needed to carry out the crime. In typical fashion, his planning was meticulous, and (he thought) accounted for every possible eventuality. Now, he decided, was the time to act.

Leslie Whittle was the seventeen-year-old daughter of George Whittle. George was a self-made man who had left the coal mines to start his own coach and bus company. The business had grown and, as a result, George became very wealthy. He was married to Selina and, although the pair had been separated for thirty years, Selina refused to divorce him. George lived with his partner, Dorothy and the couple had two children, Ronald and Lesley. The family home was a large, imposing house standing in its own grounds among others of similar design in the village of Highley, Shropshire. Upon his death in 1970, George left money and assets to the value of £250,000 (In excess of £3.4 - $4.45 million in 2022 values) which he declared was to be shared between the three of them. Selina was determined to have her share of the fortune and instigated legal proceedings to claim what she considered to be hers. Selina was eventually granted £1,500 (Just over £17,600 - $23,000 in 2022 values) plus £30 a week allowance (£352.95 - $462.88).

Neilson followed the story as it ran in the newspapers and the sums involved immediately piqued his interest. If, he thought, he could somehow get his hands on a portion of the Whittle fortune, it would be the biggest payday of his entire criminal career.

***

On January 14th 1975, Lesley Whittle returned home from college, where she was studying for her 'A' levels. Her mother, Dorothy (who had changed her surname to Whittle by deed poll some years before) had gone out for the evening, leaving Lesley in the house on her own. Around 10.15pm Ronald telephoned and they chatted for a short while.

When Dorothy Whittle returned home at about 1.15am she looked in on Lesley and found her sound asleep in bed. Satisfied all was well, she took a sleeping pill before retiring to her own room.

Less than one hour later Neilson arrived on the scene in a car he had stolen specifically for the task. He'd changed the number plates so that the vehicle (a green Austin 1100) now sported a false registration. Neilson parked the car a short distance from the house and continued the rest of the way on foot.

Once in the grounds he gained entry to the garage which adjoined the house and from there into the property itself via a side door. After climbing the stairs, Neilson was confronted with four bedroom doors; by chance the first one he elected to peer into was Lesley's.

The first thing Lesley knew of the incident was when she was shook awake and saw a hooded man armed with a sawn-off shotgun standing at her bedside. The man warned her to keep quiet before ordering her out of bed. He allowed her to put on her dressing gown and slippers before applying surgical plaster over her mouth and taping her hands together behind her back. She was then directed out of the room and down the stairs. One can only imagine what was going through her mind at this time.

She was diverted into the lounge just long enough for the man to place a ransom message, written in dymotape, on top of a chocolate box on the coffee table where it could be easily spotted. The message instructed the reader to be at a telephone box outside the Swan shopping centre in nearby Kidderminster. The person attending had to be there by 6pm that same evening and stay until 1am the following morning. There would be a phone call sometime during that period and, upon picking up the receiver, they were to answer by giving their name and saying nothing more. They were to have the ransom money with them and be prepared for further instruction. Chillingly, the message ended 'no police and no tricks otherwise death'.

The ransom demand was for £50,000 (just over £464,000 - $685,000 in 2022 values) in used notes.

After he'd placed the message, Neilson took Leslie out through the garage and down the road and, after bundling her into the back of his car and warning her to lay still, he drove off into the winter's night.

***

During his planning, and prior to the kidnap, Neilson had poured over Ordnance Survey maps of the area surrounding the Whittle's home. He'd been looking for suitable locations where Lesley could be held without fear of discovery; he'd planned from the start that he would have to leave her alone throughout much of the kidnap, therefore he knew it was imperative that the chosen site would be remote enough to prevent her being found by either chance or design.

Another vital component of his plot was to pinpoint appropriate places where the ransom money could be handed over. Given all the possibilities for compromise that entailed, Neilson had no intention of meeting the courier. He'd decided early on that the 'drop' would be done by the courier who would have been instructed to place the ransom money at a location of Neilson's choosing then leave the scene so that it could be collected shortly afterwards.

At first Neilson considered using a railway bridge as the drop point, instructing the courier to walk into the centre before dropping the money off the bridge and onto the ground below where Neilson could recover it. Another plan was to have the money thrown off a moving train as it arrived at a feature along the line of his – Neilson's – choosing.

Neilson travelled to his shortlist of locations in order to satisfy himself of their suitability. He was looking for a remote place, which couldn't easily be cordoned off by police, and where any attempt to put officers on the ground around the immediate area in order to apprehend him as he collected the ransom money would be very difficult. With his idea of receiving the money from a moving train becoming more attractive, Neilson made another study, this time concentrating on the local rail network. These subsequent map appreciations had alerted him to Bathpool Park, near Kidsgrove, Staffordshire. A high speed rail line ran alongside the park and, on paper at least, it looked like the ideal location for the drop. Neilson decided to pay a visit to the locality to carry out a detailed survey of the railway line and surrounding area. It was during this reconnaissance that he discovered Bathpool Park played host to an extensive underground overflow system which was connected to the nearby reservoir. He found one of the vertical access shafts hidden among some trees at a point where it was beyond the pathways used by dag walkers and the like. He gained entry into the shaft – and which led down to the main drainage pipes – and immediately knew this would be the ideal place in which to hold his victim.

***

After kidnapping Lesley from her bed, Neilson

drove from the Whittle home to Bathurst Park, observing the speed limits all the way lest he provoke the attention of any police patrol cars. He'd put the shotgun in the boot but was still armed, the .22 pistol hidden beneath his coat, ready to be drawn if required. There is absolutely no doubt that had he been routinely stopped by the police – who weren't aware of the crime he was committing – he would have opened fire.

Once at the park, Neilson left his vehicle in one of the secluded car parks and led Lesley towards their destination. It was still early, far too early to run the risk of bumping into dog walkers, so Neilson was confident that he wouldn't be seen.

Opening the inspection hatch, and after untying the girl, he ordered her to climb down into the shaft before following behind on the metal ladder. Some sixty-five feet below the surface they came to a narrow ledge where, by torchlight, Neilson ordered Lesley to climb into a sleeping bag. After giving her a torch and a flask of hot soup, Neilson tied a wire noose around her neck in such a manner that it could not be undone, leaving her with very little room for manoeuvre and warning her that if she attempted to free herself she would fall and be garrotted.

With that, Neilson left Leslie, terrified and alone in the darkness. His mission now was to collect the £50,000.

***

When she woke the following morning, Dorothy prepared breakfast then took Lesley's up to her room. It was 6.50am and still dark.

Dorothy turned on the electric fire before moving across the room to wake her daughter. It was then she realised Lesley was not in bed. At that stage she thought little of it and simply shouted to tell Lesley that her breakfast was served. When there was no reply, Dorothy looked around the room. Lesley's clothes were still hanging where she always left them, ready to put on the following day. After checking the bathroom, Dorothy decided to telephone her son, Ronald, but the telephone was out of order (she was unaware that Neilson had cut the line). Bewildered by events, Dorothy decided to get in her car and take the short drive to Ronald's house. When she explained what had happened, Ronald suggested that Lesley may just have gone to college early, but Dorothy pointed out that her clothes were still hanging up.

Ronald accompanied his mother back to the house and together they tried to make sense of the situation, it was shortly afterwards, when they were looking to make sure Lesley hadn't left an explanatory note, that the ransom demand was found.

After reading the dymotape message and realising what was happening, Ronald made the decision to ignore the warning and contact the police.

Detective Chief Superintendent Bob Booth was head of West Mercia CID. He was a career policeman with a long and impressive track record. During his time with the CID, Det Ch Supt Booth had solved every one of the seventy murder cases he'd investigated and recently been awarded an MBE in recognition of the fact. He was due to retire from the police and preparing to take up a senior position within the British security services.

He'd been alerted to the news about Lesley's abduction soon after Ronald made contact with the police and was driven to the scene in an unmarked car. With the warning on the dymo tape message at the forefront of his mind, as far as Det Ch Supt Booth concerned he wanted to keep the police involvement as covert as possible for the time being just in case the Whittle home was under some sort of surveillance.

Arriving at the house he was met by Dorothy and Ronald. They were both obviously upset by the unfolding incident and Booth was particularly struck by how distraught Dorothy was, in fact, he later remarked that he'd never seen anyone as upset at having one of their children missing in his life.

Det Ch Supt Booth set to work. His first priority was to react to the contents of the note and to Ronald's insistence that the ransom should be paid and he – Ronald – himself would act as courier. Booth knew the kidnapper hadn't given him much time to formulate a coordinated response, he also must assume that whoever was responsible would take it for granted that the police would be involved. The fact that that the dymotape message also clearly stipulated that 'any tricks' or police would result in Lesley's death worried him greatly. He had no way of knowing if this was a hollow threat, but it was imperative that he took the warning seriously and that, he knew, would set the tone for the coming operation.

Det Ch Supt Booth had a couple of his plain clothed men visit the Whittle's bank where they withdrew £50,000 in used notes from Dorothy's account. The money was then taken to police headquarters where it was photocopied. Given the tight deadline set by the kidnapper, the CID didn't have time to individually record the each note's serial number, so did them this way – in bulk – in order that they could be taken down afterwards. By archiving the details of each note, the police would then be able to track them all as they appeared. Where and how they were spent could lead to narrowing down the field of search for the perpetrator and – possibly – a description. If they were very lucky the purchase of an item which required a guarantee (something like a TV for example) could yield a name and address. *In the 1970s CCTV systems were unheard of outside institutions such as banks, so there was virtually no chance of the kidnapper being caught on camera as he spent the money. Even if he was, many security cameras were of low resolution and not linked to recording devices.*

The only firm piece of information Det Ch Supt Booth had to go on was the telephone box at the Swan shopping centre. It was entirely possible, he reasoned, that the kidnapper might make an appearance to take the money in person. With that in mind he issued orders for a team of plain clothed detectives to be assembled.

At police headquarters, Booth briefed his men. They were to insert themselves at various locations surrounding the telephone box from where they could mount a covert operation to keep it under observation and apprehend the suspect should he make an appearance. Support units were to be at the ready in unmarked cars should they be needed and, working on the assumption that the perpetrator was armed, everyone involved who were firearms trained was issued with revolvers. Booth was keen to stress that it was imperative that the suspect be captured and, unless their own lives were in immediate danger, guns were to be kept holstered. He wanted the kidnapper alive and able to talk, otherwise he had no possibility of finding Lesley.

Booth also ordered that marked police units be kept out of the area during the times given on the dymotape ransom message, if the kidnapper was indeed intending to show up he didn't want him spooked by the sight of a random police patrol.

***

The undercover units were trickle fed into position that afternoon. Det Ch Supt Booth wanted them in place long before the suspect might show up to put the place under observation of his own.

Darkness falls early in February in the UK but the sun had yet to set before the police were ready and waiting.

Back at the Whittle home, Ronald had been briefed about what to expect when making the drop by a couple of detectives who had brought the money to him. The cash was placed in a suitcase. He was to travel to the scene alone in his Scimitar sports car and, as instructed on the Dymotape, wait in the telephone booth until the phone rang. It would simply be a case of playing it by ear from then on. He was advised to make sure his car was topped up with petrol in case he was going to get 'bounced around' by the kidnapper. His being ordered to go to another location would result in his being shadowed by CID officers in their unmarked cars. The detectives were used to this and everyone involved was confident that they could tail Ronald without being spotted. The trick was not to get too close to the vehicle being followed and to coordinate the operation so that the unmarked cars would peel off at regular intervals and be replaced by others who could immediately take up the pursuit. In built up areas, the 'swapping cars' tactic worked well, but out on single lane country roads there was always little or no opportunity to carry it out. However, the police had another trick up their sleeve.

Beside eyes on the ground, the police had dispatched Detective Inspector Eddie Barry to the telephone exchange in Kidderminster. His job was to monitor all incoming calls to the target telephone box and the one adjoining it. He was issued with a tape machine upon which he'd record the calls. As an extra precaution, a listening watch was also mounted on other public telephones in and around the Swan Shopping centre in case the kidnapper happened to make any calls from those. If Ronald was told to travel on from the telephone box, the police would be able to descend upon his destination and thereafter have an opportunity to make an arrest.

Ronald arrived on the scene at the appointed time with the case full of money. He entered the telephone box and waited.
There in the shadows, hiding in buildings, the police also waited. Their radios were ready to pick up transmissions should the kidnapper be spotted and their eyes scanned the scene in the hope of being the first to see the target.

Det Ch Supt Booth thought he had covered every angle and he almost had. However, while he thought he'd managed to keep the kidnapping of Lesley quiet, he had overlooked the need to request a news blackout on the story so, at more or less the exact same time as Ronald was arriving at the telephone box, news of the abduction broke across the radio and television.

Back at the police operations room, Det Ch Supt Butler was astonished when he was told that the media were broadcasting details of the kidnap. From the initial bulletins it was obvious they had precise information about the crime, including Lesley's name and the amount being demanded.

Unwittingly, Butler knew, and if the threats contained within the ransom were genuine, this may well result in Lesley's death.

Weighing up the situation then making a decision quickly, Butler decided to press on with the operation in the hope that, somehow, the kidnapper may not have heard the news.

Unaware of the unfolding situation, Ronald waited in the telephone box. As the hours ticked by the police became convinced that the operation had been blown, but they were wrong. Neilson had been too busy to listen to the radio so was unaware that his crime was being broadcast on every bulletin. At around midnight

– some six hours after Ronald had first arrived at the telephone box – Neilson made the call.

Over at the telephone exchange, Det Insp Barry was alerted to the call and turned on the tape recorder in readiness to document what was said. To his surprise, the telephone rang without being answered until the caller hung up. He was perplexed and immediately contacted Det Ch Supt Booth to tell him what had happened. Booth then contacted the surveillance team and was angered to learn that there had been a mix up in communication somewhere between them and him resulting in the officer in charge at the scene calling off the operation when he learned of the news leak. He'd instructed Ronald Whittle to return home so there was no one to take the call.
Booth was incandescent. This was a grave error and one he feared which would cost Lesley her life. The fact that he felt he had personally let Lesley down was communicated to all those involved in a most forceful manner. He knew that time and fortune was now against him, he would have to think and act quickly if he was to save Lesley and rescue the situation.

***

As the kidnap of Lesley Whittle entered its second day a media circus descended upon Highley. The story was headline news across the TV and radio, while newspaper coverage was running into multiple pages per edition. Reporters and photographers thronged through the streets in an attempt to pick up scraps of gossip or hitherto unknown facts. Some were even going door to door in their quest for information.

For obvious reasons, the main focus of attention lay on Dorothy and Ronald Whittle and the press were desperate to interview them. For his part, Det Ch Supt Booth was keen to keep them away from the media. While Ronald was managing to remain composed, the same couldn't be said for Dorothy, She was in obvious distress and Booth knew her agonies would be compounded by press intrusion.

Aside from trying to protect the Whittle's from the media, Booth had other, more pressing, matters on his mind. Secretly, he feared that the kidnapper may have already carried out his threat to murder Lesley; after all, it was obvious that the police were now fully involved. He had no way of making contact with the person responsible other than to make a public appeal to him via the news people, but he was loathed to do that. Instead he took the unusual decision to return to the telephone box in the scant hope the kidnapper may try to call again. Booth realised it was a long shot, a very long shot indeed, but he was prepared to give it a try.

Ronald was contacted and agreed to visit the telephone box again that night. Det Ch Supt Booth knew neither he nor Dorothy had spoken to the press, and were unlikely to in the coming days, yet he impressed upon Ronald the need for secrecy in order to give his plan a chance to work.

Once again the undercover police team was assembled and put into place around the telephone box. There was little hope of the kidnapper making an appearance, but Booth wanted to be prepared just in case. Ronald was taken from the Whittle home in the back of an unmarked police van and, as a result, managed to evade the attention of the waiting media. He then drove himself to the scene and entered the telephone box. He hadn't been there long when a crowd of reporters and photographers appeared. They crowded around the telephone box, taking photographs and asking questions. The police watched on with incredulity as the press mob attempted to draw Ronald into conversation. Det Ch Supt Booth was quickly informed of the development and he was not happy. How had the press got wind of his plan? He was asked if the police should move in and disperse the press men but he said no, it would mean breaking cover and giving the fact that they were waiting to trap the kidnapper; if he just happened to be observing the scene, or the press started taking photographs of plain clothed police to report it in next day's newspapers, it would almost definitely result in Lesley's death.

In the event, Ronald waited several hours, all the time being harassed by the press. Perhaps predictably, there was no incoming phone call so he returned home with the pack of reporters in tow.

By this time Det Ch Supt Booth's anger was boiling over. He was convinced that the actions of the press had placed Lesley in mortal danger. The clock was ticking. He had to find her before time ran out.

***

On the third day of the kidnap, the police were no closer to finding Lesley or her captor. During this time, poor Lesley had been in the drainage shaft alone and frightened. She was unable to move for fear of stumbling and falling. In the freezing cold and pitch blackness all she could hear was the trickle of water through the overflow pipe some distance below and the squeaking and scuttling of rats. Words cannot describe how terrifying it must have been for her.

That night, at midnight, the telephone rang at the home of Len Rudd, the then transport manager at the family's coach and bus company and a close friend of the Whittle's. Len was one of a handful of people Det Ch Supt Booth had identified as possibly being on the kidnapper's contact list and as such he'd been briefed by detectives on how to react if he was called by the man holding Lesley. (Booth had gotten a feel for the way the kidnapper was thinking and correctly guessed that he wouldn't try to telephone the Whittle house lest the line was being monitored and the call traced).

Len picked up the receiver and was shocked to hear Lesley's voice. He quickly realised that it was a recorded message. Addressing her mum, Lesley said that 'you need to go to Kidsgrove post office telephone box. The instructions are inside'. She went on to say that she was 'okay' and ended the message by repeating the warning on the dymotape that 'but there are to be no police and no tricks, okay?'

Len didn't have a pen and paper to hand, so missed the details; fortunately the message was repeated, enabling him to make a note of what was said.

Immediately the call ended, Len did as he'd been instructed and telephoned the police.

From his perspective, the cautious Neilson had made provision should his initial plan to have the ransom money delivered go wrong and, now that he was fully aware that news of his crime had broken, he was able to fall back on his contingency.

Det Ch Supt Booth was at home when he took a telephone call from police headquarters, alerting him to this important development. He was immediately excited. It not only meant that Lesley was still probably still alive, but it gave him the chance to get his operation back onto the front foot. The kidnapper, he guessed, was far too deep into his plot to allow the chance of collecting the £50,000 to pass him by. It was this desire to come into possession of the money which might prove the break the police were looking for.

Given the national publicity surrounding the case, it had been decided by Booth's superiors to draft in a specialist surveillance team from the Metropolitan Police. It was a wise decision, as these officers possessed skills which Booth's own team simply did not have.

Kidsgrove post office was just north of Stoke – on-Trent, some seventy-five miles away from the Whittle home. Booth knew it was vital to make it appear that Ronald Whittle – who had once again volunteered to deliver the ransom – was acting alone. Time was short; the kidnapper had given only two hours from receipt of the telephone call to the deadline for the drop. Hurriedly, the Met team met with Ronald and fitted him with a hi-tech body worn radio transmitter. The device was covert and could transmit on a preset frequency to officers within a radius of a mile or so. All Ronald had to do was speak and his voice would be picked up. He was briefed on what to do while carrying out the drop. It was vital, he was told, that he keep the police informed of any instructions he was given as he received them; this would allow the unmarked units who were shadowing Ronald at beyond visual range, to react accordingly. Ronald was also assured that the police would be able to provide assistance, should he require it, within two minutes of him requesting help.

Because the drop was due to take place in neighbouring Staffordshire, Det Ch Supt Booth made contact with that police force to warn them what was happening. He explained that the forthcoming operation was of a very delicate nature and requested that local police units stay clear of the area around Kidsgrove.

At 1.30am, Ronald left Bridgenorth police station and commenced the drive north to Kidsgrove. It was only ninety minutes since the recorded message from Lesley had been received but he was already running late. Det Ch Supt Booth knew the kidnapper was acting deliberately by not allowing any time for the money to be delivered; the less time allowed, the less time the police (if the Whittle's had involved them) would be able to formulate a plan of action.

Ronald arrived late at Kidsgrove post office; he was unfamiliar with the area and had become lost after taking a couple of wrong turns. He left his car and entered the telephone box to begin his search for the set of instructions he'd been told were there. Try as he might he simply could not find any hidden messages. Was the whole thing a hoax? Since the story of Lesley's abduction broke and her photograph appeared across the press and TV news there had been multiple sightings of her phoned in to West Mercia Police. Obviously done with the best of intentions, as each one had to be followed up, these same reports only served to use precious police resources. Sickeningly, there had also been several hoax calls from people claiming to be the kidnapper, either demanding the ransom money or simply passing false information about Lesley's whereabouts and state of health. These too had to be treated seriously and took officers away from the real investigation.

No, Ronald knew, the phone call Len Rudd had taken was definitely the real thing. He'd reported that the voice on the line was undoubtedly that of Lesley, who he knew well. In desperation Ronald telephoned the incident room at West Mercia Police and was told to look again.

All in all it took Ron half an hour before he found the dymotape message. It had been so well hidden behind the backboard (a notice board which was a feature off all public telephones and held various information relating to the operation of the payphone, plus useful numbers, etc) as to be rendered almost invisible. On the tape were instructions which directed Ronald to another rendezvous. Speaking softly in the knowledge that his words were being transmitted to unseen police units, Ronald read out the message. 'GO TO THE TOP OF THE LANE AND TURN INTO NO ENTRY GO TO THE WALL AND FLASH LIGHTS LOOK FOR TORCHLIGHT RUN TO TORCH FURTHER INSTRUCTIONS ON TORCH' before setting off into the darkness once more

He'd been directed to Bathpool Park and, as instructed, turned through into the car park then along a lane at the far side. The 'wall' which Neilson mentioned was in fact the wall over a railway bridge. It was pitch black and, because the bridge itself curves into a left-hand sweep, Ronald completely missed it in his headlights as they were shining towards the apex of the curve, as a result he continued slowly along the lane. A short distance later he came to the dam at the edge of the Bathpool reservoir and, assuming that this was the wall alluded to in the dymotape message, stopped and began to flash his headlights. He was now about a quarter of a mile beyond the intended rendezvous point with no way of knowing that he'd missed his mark.

Ronald waited for an hour with no sign of the torch beam signal. Finally realising that the kidnapper wasn't going to show, he retired the couple of miles to a pre-arranged rendezvous with the police. Everyone was at a loss to understand what had gone wrong as they drove back south.

***

The next morning the West Mercia police were keen to establish what had gone wrong. Both they and the Metropolitan team were adamant that the kidnapper could not have spotted them, by virtue of the fact that they had steered well clear of the immediate area, relying instead on Ronald's running commentary as he followed the details on the dymotape message. Rather than anything the police or Ronald had done to spook the kidnapper, they concluded that he hadn't shown up through some fault of his own. With that in mind, they were confident that he would make contact again soon to rearrange the drop.

In part, the police were correct, Neilson hadn't seen them, but left the scene after a series of unconnected incidents convinced him the area was under surveillance before Ronald arrived.

At around the time Ronald was due to arrive at Bathurst Park, a local man and his girlfriend drove into the car park, close to where the ransom drop was be made. He's been working as a DJ in a nearby nightclub and decided to stop at the park before dropping his girlfriend off at her home. As they sat in the car they suddenly saw a torch flashing in the distance. The couple thought it odd that someone should be walking in the park at that time of night but decided it was someone out exercising their dog and thought no more of it. Shortly afterwards a police panda car drove into the car park and stopped only a few yards from the couple's car. As soon as this marked vehicle hove into view the torchlight was extinguished. The occupants of both vehicles could see each other quite clearly and it soon became obvious to the couple that the PC in the panda car had come into the park for a smoke break. The couple left shortly thereafter thinking no more of the strange incident with the torch.

Watching from the trees, Neilson must have mistaken the courting couple for Ronald Whittle and – despite the car not identifying itself by flashing its headlights – he began to wave his torch in the recognition signal as he said he would. The car park was empty and had been all the while Neilson was there so, at that moment he (Neilson) probably though Ronald had simply forgotten about his own signal. The sudden and unexpected arrival of a marked police car on the scene would have immediately set him thinking that the police were in the process of springing a trap.

As far as Neilson was concerned he now had to leave the area before it could be cordoned off and searched. He'd already planned out his escape route in the event of such a move by the police, making use of the best available ground cover and topographical features he knew offered the best chance of evading any police search.

As he was withdrawing, Neilson heard a light

aircraft overhead. This was the final straw and convinced him that the police were converging on the park to cordon it off then hunt him down. In actual fact, the aircraft was simply on a routine flight and a civilian, not police, plane. Given what he thought was happening on the ground around him, Neilson needed no encouragement to tie it in with his imagined predicament.

As all this was happening, Lesley remained trapped in the shaft. Alone in the pitch blackness, freezing cold, and with no prospect of help, she must have been terrified. Though she wasn't to know it, the chances of her being found were rapidly dwindling.

***

Frustrated by the night's events, Det Ch Supt Booth wanted to make a large scale search of Bathpool Park, utilising all the resources available to him. He suspected that Lesley may be being held somewhere in the vicinity and this could be the police's only opportunity to find her. Mooting his plan to other senior officers, he ran into opposition from the Met team. They said that it was still too early in the investigation to carry out such an action as they had no idea if the kidnapper thought the police were actually involved in the matter. To flood Bathpool Park with police would only confirm they were and, with the ransom message warnings in mind, could lead to Lesley's death. Booth wasn't happy as he was confident the suspect would already know he was being hunted by the police so, as a compromise, he was told that a team of plain clothed officers from the Met would carry out a search of the park. They'd be able to work without bringing attention to themselves or what they were doing.

That same day small unit of Metropolitan Police detectives arrived at Bathpool Park to begin what they considered to be a thorough yet discreet search of the area for clues as to where Lesley might be being held.

At Staffordshire Police Headquarters, news of the abortive ransom drop began to filter through to senior officers. Amazingly not one of them had any idea what Det Ch Sup Booth's team were doing on their 'patch'. The request from West Mercia Police for the Staffordshire constabulary to 'stay in bed' had not gone beyond anyone of junior rank. The Head of Staffordshire CID, Detective Chief Superintendent Harold Wright, was suitably angry at the fact that he was unaware of events and local police – police with intimate knowledge of the area – had been shut out of the operation.

After making a few inquiries it transpired that Ronald Whittle was not the only one to lose his way along the tangle of dark country roads which bisected the locality. The officers following on behind Ronald had also become lost and were forced to contact the information room at police HQ, Stafford, and ask for directions to Kidsgrove. Later on, more calls were put in to the information room to ask for advice on how to get from Kidsgrove to Bathpool Park.

Det Ch Supt Wright was quite correct when he stated that, had local officers been involved in the operation, there would have been no delays stemming from confusion about routes and, probably, the drop would have taken place as planned. Had that then resulted in Lesley being released or directions to where she was hidden being given is a matter for debate, but the fact remained that any prospect of her being rescued that night had evaporated.

Bathpool Park covers 178 acres, so the small Metropolitan Police search team had little hope of covering the area effectively. Unfamiliar with the surroundings, on the first day of their investigation of the park, they failed to spot the potential significance of the overflow system's inspection shafts. As will be explained in due course, this search was to prove another bone of contention between Staffordshire and West Mercia police.

In the event, the Met team spent two days looking for clues in the park before concluding that the area was of no significance to the inquiry. How close they came to where Lesley had been imprisoned, no one will ever know.

***

While the search of Bathpool Park was ongoing, Ronald Whittle received an anonymous telephone call at the family home. By this time, the police had set up tape recorders on the lines of all those they deemed may be contacted by the kidnapper, as well as the ability to record any calls and – possibly – capture the voice of the wanted man on tape, working with the telephone company the police had also (with the knowledge of those involved) the ability to trace any incoming telephone calls. The duration of the call Ronald took was to too short for the location to be pinpointed and the only information the police were able to glean was that it originated from Gloucestershire.

Unlike the other calls which had come in over the past few days, both Ronald and the detectives on the scene thought it to be genuine; therefore preparations were immediately put in place to carry out the instructions as specified by the unknown caller.

After a flurry of communication between the detectives on scene and West Mercia Police HQ, Ronald set out with the suitcase of money to make the drop. He was being tailed by undercover officers in unmarked cars who were hoping to arrive on the scene then place themselves around it to contain the area and, after the money was handed over, effect an arrest. It soon became clear that the media had gotten wind of the operation and – incredibly – a convoy of press and TV reporters fell in behind Ronald and the unmarked police cars. When Det Ch Supt Booth was informed of this development he hit the roof. How could the media be so stupid as to endanger such a delicate police operation and, by association, Lesley's life?

According to the telephone call, the ransom money was to be handed over at a junction on the M5 motorway. Det Ch Supt Booth was convinced that the location had been chosen because it offered the kidnapper uninterrupted views along the motorway and the roads leading to the junction itself, therefore, he'd be able to spot anyone who was following Ronald Whittle as he made his approach.

Booth knew he had to do something if he was to stop the press from jeopardising the situation so immediately put in a call to order the interdiction of the press vehicles by traffic police and, controversially, the closure of the motorway itself so none of them were able to recommence the chase at another junction. The convoy of press vehicles was intercepted and brought to a halt as it made to follow Ronald on to the motorway, leaving the drop to continue without hindrance. In the event, the telephone call proved to be yet another elaborate hoax. It seemed that the real kidnapper had gone silent.

As if to rub salt into his wounds details began to emerge of what had happened in and around

Bathpool Park on the night of the abortive ransom drop. Staffordshire Police were adamant that none of their officers or vehicles had been in the vicinity of the park that night. The account given by the DJ was also firmly denied. After first presuming that the couple had been mistaken when they claimed they saw a police panda car, Staffordshire CID later said that if they had, it definitely wasn't one belonging to the local force.

Privately, the recriminations continued to fly and intensified when Det Ch Supt Booth came into possession of a telex message from Staffordshire Police, detailing the registration numbers of vehicles which had been in the area surrounding Kidsgrove and Bathpool Park. As well as Ronald Whittle's Scimitar, the list contained the details of the Metropolitan Police's surveillance vehicles and others belonging to West Mercia's Crime Squad (who were being held off from getting too close to the actual drop and there to provide backup should it be required). As far as he was concerned it was proof that Staffordshire Police had ignored his request that they 'stay in bed' and instead carried out a containment operation of their own to check out all vehicles which were out and about on the roads that night.

***

The next couple of days passed without further incident. With his mind focused on the return of

Lesley, Det Ch Supt Booth was desperate to make contact with a kidnapper who had now stopped issuing ransom demands. It was obvious to everyone involved that any further attempt to make it appear that the police weren't involved in the case was pointless so, after speaking with the Whittle's, he persuaded them to take part in a public appeal. The object of the exercise was to directly communicate with the kidnapper in the hope of prompting him to re-establish contact. In the event, the Whittle's made several appearances on TV and radio, while also speaking at length to all the press. Ronald stressed that the family had been subjected to numerous bogus telephone calls and would only deal with the actual kidnapper upon receipt of evidence that Lesley was alive and well. This, it was hoped, would prompt the kidnapper into making another recording of Lesley's voice.

Unfortunately, this latest ploy by Det Ch Supt Booth failed to yield any results. By this time, and still believing that any attempt to collect the ransom money would be met by a police sting operation, Neilson had decided to abandon the kidnap. The details of what happened to Leslie after the bungled attempt to deliver the money at Bathpool Park are still debatable. The only people who ever knew the truth were Lesley and Neilson. One school of thought has it that after retiring from the scene in a fit of rage, Neilson returned to the draining shaft and pushed Lesley to her death. Another theory is that Lesley was left abandoned and fell by accident from the ledge. Whichever version of events you believe it is still obvious that Neilson was directly responsible for the poor girl's death.

It's the author's opinion that in his haste to escape what he believed to be a police operation to capture him, Neilson wouldn't have returned to the access shaft to kill Lesley. His priority would have been simply to make good his own escape. The previous incidents, as recorded earlier in this book, clearly show he was a man possessed of little compassion; a ruthless killer who had no thought for anyone but himself. (Of course, Neilson could well have returned the following night to kill Lesley but, given that he must assume police were still on the scene, would he?)

If this was how events played out, when he'd decided to abort any further attempts to collect the ransom money, there was nothing to stop him from alerting the authorities as to Lesley's whereabouts so that she could be rescued and returned home. There was no need for Neilson to contact the police directly, He could have sent another dymotape message to the press – posting it from the West Midlands area to avoid giving away any clues. That he didn't speaks volumes about his character and his utter disregard for human life. As far as Neilson was concerned, Lesley was simply a commodity; a commodity to be traded for cash. When – his in eyes – she was no longer of value to him she could be discarded like any other 'disposable' item without second thought or flicker of empathy.

***

The police operation to find Lesley had stalled. Over the course of the next week it became clear that, despite the public appeals by the Whittle's, the kidnapper had no intention of pursuing his ransom demands.

Six days after the unsuccessful ransom drop at Bathpool Park, Det Ch Supt Booth was contacted by West Midlands Police. A car had been abandoned in a car park in Dudley, just three-hundred yards from the scene of a shooting which had occurred a few days before.

The vehicle in question, a green Austin 1100 with the registration number TTV454H, had caught the eye of a local resident who thought it suspicious and reported it to the police. After making a cursory visual inspection of the car, West Midlands CID immediately suspected the vehicle may have some connection to the Lesley Whittle kidnapping. A call was made to West Mercia Police to ask if Det Ch Supt Booth would care to examine it.

Booth's driver ferried him up to the scene in an unmarked car. Wishing to preserve evidence if the car was found to have some connection to the kidnap of Lesley, it was left where it had been found. With the car park sealed off, Booth set to work. During his initial inspection, just by briefly looking through the windows, it was immediately obvious that the vehicle had not simply been stolen then dumped after being used in some routine crime. On display, scattered around the interior, were several items which piqued Booth's interest. A length of rope was curled around the vicinity of the gearstick and, most chillingly of all, a cassette recorder was sitting on the front passenger seat. Booth agreed with his West Midlands' colleagues and the car was recovered to a police compound where a detailed forensic examination could take place. The recorder was found to contain a cassette which, after being dusted for fingerprints, was delivered to Booth. When played, the cassette contained a recording of Lesley Whittle's voice directing the listener to a telephone box off junction ten of the M6 and thereafter to a telephone box where, Lesley said, instructions were 'taped under the shelf of a telephone box.'

Det Ch Supt Booth's heart sank. He knew he'd lost valuable time by not having the vehicle which had been used to kidnap Lesley found earlier. The car yielded more evidence in the form of four envelopes which each gave details of a ransom run to four telephone boxes in different parts of the West Midlands. Booth quickly realised that the dymotape notes were significant as they gave details of the route to have been used on the first night of the kidnap, when Ronald Whittle waited at the telephone box at the Swan shopping centre.

Booth climbed into the front passenger seat of his unmarked car and had his driver follow the instructions to the first telephone box. There, as Lesley intimated during her recording, taped out of sight, was a dymotape message.

The notes would have led Ronald on a circuitous journey, bouncing at tangents from telephone box to telephone box to his final destination; another telephone box just yards from the car park where the kidnapper's car was found abandoned. Booth followed the trail all the way to the car park. The final set of instructions directed him to drive across the bridge to the nearby Freightliner depot.

A police search of the area quickly revealed another length of dymotape fixed to a telegraph pole. It read 'cross road onto car park to gate eight of Dudley zoo'. This was very close to where the shooting had taken place. Booth wanted to know every detail of that incident and was briefed by the senior West Midlands CID officer in charge of investigating it.

At the same time as Ronald Whittle was spending that second night waiting at the Swan shopping centre telephone box, Neilson was at Dudley zoo, making final preparations for the drop. He had no idea why Ronald hadn't taken his telephone call, but decided to try again. His plan was to lay in wait for Ronald behind gate eight. Another dymotape message was fixed to the gate itself and instructed Ronald to tie the suitcase to a rope which was hanging over the gate. Once this was done, and Ronald had retreated beyond visual range, Neilson intended to recover the case by simply hauling it up and over the gate. Given the fact that the area was unlit and the only illumination was very weak overspill from the neighbouring Freightliner depot, he knew he could carry out this operation unseen, thereafter quickly making good his escape through the zoo and out into open country beyond. The fact that both the gate and zoo walls were high enough to stop anyone climbing over into the zoo also meant that any police who were intent on apprehending Neilson would not have been able to get to him.

Gerald Smith was on duty that night. Gerald was a security officer at the Dudley Freightliner depot. As part of his duties he would undertake patrols of the site to make sure no one was attempting to break in or otherwise cause trouble. A memo had been circulated among the security staff warning them to be on the alert for suspicious activity, as the IRA were active on the mainland at that time and the Freightliner depot has been identified as a potential target by the authorities.

It was while on routine foot patrol that Gerald spotted a man acting suspiciously in the vicinity of Dudley zoo. Gerald decided to follow the man to make sure he wasn't going to enter Freightliner property. It quickly became clear that the stranger had seen Gerald and was attempting to evade him. Before long, Gerald had seen enough. He hadn't challenged the stranger but instead simply turned away to return to the security office and phone the police. All of a sudden two shots, fired in quick succession, cut through the night air. Gerald stumbled then fell, having taken both rounds in the back. As he lay face up on the ground the man approached and casually levelled the pistol before emptying what remained in the magazine into the helpless Gerald.

Amazingly, Gerald survived (though he was to later die as a result of the damage done to his vital organs by the gunshots). After being found he was rushed by ambulance to a nearby hospital.

It was here, a week later, that Det Ch Supt Booth interviewed him. Booth had already read the statement given by Gerald to the detectives investigating the case but wanted to see for himself if there was any more information to be had. Gerald repeated what he'd said in his witness statement. The man looked like a tramp and, although he wasn't wearing any type of face covering, the darkness and the stress of the situation meant he wasn't able to give a detailed description of his attacker's features. What Booth found most disturbing of all was how Gerald described what happened when he fell to the ground after being shot. As he lay there he watched his attacker approach until he was standing over him before coolly levelling the pistol and opening fire. Gerald said that the man responsible seemed to be enjoying the act of committing what he believed to be murder. Another thing which Gerald said deeply disturbed Det Ch Supt Booth; when he'd emptied the magazine's worth of ammunition into him, the gunman kept on squeezing the trigger in an attempt to fire more rounds. Gerald was convinced that, had his attacker been carrying another magazine, he would have reloaded and emptied it into him. After the shooting, the man had disappeared towards the zoo car park. At this point his victim was still conscious but the gunman must have been sure he'd delivered fatal injuries.

Despite being severely wounded, Gerald managed to stumble back to the security office from where he called the police.

Once in hospital he underwent emergency surgery. One of his kidneys had to be removed and his liver was found to be badly damaged.

Booth had little doubt that the man responsible and the kidnapper were one and the same and Gerald's account meant he was looking for someone who wouldn't hesitate to kill. Given all which had happened over the past week, he silently feared that the culprit would have no hesitation in killing Lesley.

***

When forensic examination of the bullets fired into Gerald Smith were analysed by forensic experts, as a matter of routine the results were cross referenced against bullets of the same calibre which had been recovered from other crimes. The forensics people uncovered evidence which was to shock not only the police, but the whole nation. The .22 rounds used in the Smith shooting had been fired from the same gun as the one used to kill Donald Skepper, Derek Astin and Sidney Grayland. Given his usually meticulous precautions, the small size of .22 long rifle cartridges meant they couldn't be loaded while wearing gloves; the result being there were also enough fragments of fingerprints on the spent cartridges left at the scene of all four crimes to establish that the same gunman was responsible.

When news reached Det Ch Supt Booth it was like a blow to the solar plexus. The man who had kidnapped Lesley Whittle was none other than the notorious Black Panther.

News that the man police were hunting for in the Lesley Whittle case was Britain's most wanted robber quickly leaked to the press and a media storm quickly ensued. The story not only made headline news across the UK but the rest of the world. Lesley was still missing and concerns for her safety were magnified when this latest revelation came to the surface. With the media spotlight still firmly on the kidnapping, the pressure was on the police to find Lesley and bring her home – fast.

For his part, at first Neilson must have been shocked that the police had tied him to the kidnapping. However, and in the knowledge that he'd left nothing in his wake which could possibly lead detectives to uncover his identity, he remained sure that he'd once again successfully evaded justice.

Meanwhile, Lesley (or her body) remained where he'd abandoned her.

***

Det Ch Supt Booth was clinging on the belief that Lesley may just still be alive and with that at the forefront of his mind, he decided to act.
The Black Panther, whoever he was, had stopped trying to make contact with the Whittle's and appeared to have abandoned his ransom demands, but – Booth surmised – there was still need for him to exercise caution. He wanted to mount a full-scale search of Bathpool Park, as his instincts were telling him that Lesley may be somewhere within its precincts. However, and just in case the Black Panther was holding Lesley

somewhere else and such an obvious search may put her in jeopardy, he would have to be even more cunning as the man he was hunting.

Booth approached Ronald Whittle with his plan and he agreed to participate. No one else was to be privy to what was to transpire as security was paramount to its success.

Under Det Ch Supt Booth's direction, Ronald took part in a TV news documentary about Lesley's kidnap. During his interview, Ronald (intentionally) let slip that he'd carried out a ransom run to Kidsgrove and Bathpool Park. Afterwards, the TV crew interviewed Det Ch Supt Booth and the following is a transcript of that exchange which took place:

Reporter: "Are you going to have to go for this man if he contacts Ronnie Whittle again?"

Booth: "Pardon? Again?"

Reporter: "Yes."

Booth: "What do you mean, again?"

Reporter: "Whittle says he's already made a contact. I thought you might have known about this?"

Booth: "But I don't know about it until you've

just raised it. How did you get to know about it?"

Reporter: "Well, we spoke to Whittle yesterday and he mentioned, he said it was the first time he'd mentioned it to the press and, er, I wasn't quite clear that he'd mentioned it to you."

Booth: "Are you telling me now that Ron Whittle has been out somewhere, dealing with a man he believes to be the kidnapper? Is that what you're saying?"

Reporter: "Well I'm not telling you, I'm simply saying that's what Ronnie Whittle told me."

Booth: "Well then, I'm afraid this has got to terminate."

An indignant Booth finished the interview on the spot. It had been a sterling performance. The news' crew went away with what they thought was the scoop of the whole crime while Booth sat back to wait while the rest of the media, the nation and – most importantly of all – the Black Panther, swallowed the bait.

The following day, while the story was splashed across the TV news, police descended on Bathpool Park in force. If the rouse had worked, the Black Panther would be fooled into thinking Det Ch Supt Booth had legitimate reasons to conduct a search of the area.

The search was soon to uncover several items of importance which had been missed by the Metropolitan Police team during their own covert sweep of the park. A segment of dymotape which read 'drop money into hole' was found discarded next to a land drain. A spanner, used to remove the bolts on a section of bars which formed the drain cover the drain cover (that section of bars themselves had also been left wide open) and a torch upon which the dymotape message had originally been fixed were also unearthed.

Det Ch Supt Booth was angry that this evidence had lain undiscovered for so long and that much of his planning had centred around the fact that he'd been assured that there was nothing of significance within the park by the Met search team. He was convinced that, had he not been over-ridden when he wanted to first search Bathpool Park, he could have moved the investigation on and – possibly – found out where Lesley was being held. What really galled Booth was the fact that the items so far uncovered were not hidden, simply discarded. He later commented that anyone walking – not searching – the park would have found the evidence. The effectiveness, or lack thereof, of the Met operation was laid bare for all to see.

For their part, Staffordshire Police were quite rightly angry that the Met had undertaken the initial search. It stood to reason that local officers, wearing plain clothes so as not to arouse suspicion, were far better placed to mount a survey of the area. They knew the lay of the land and could have easily identified areas of possible interest even before arriving on the scene.

As the search continued, members of the public who used the park for recreation began to hand over items they themselves had found. At the time none of the people in question had any inkling that they could be tied to the Lesley Whittle case.

Given that the clues were all pointing to the land drain, Staffordshire Police Detective Constable Philip Maskery was drafted in to conduct a search of the interior of the drain. Maskery was an experienced officer who was working with the Scenes of Crime department, so possessed the skills necessary to uncover, record and preserve evidence.

Det Con Maskery was briefed then lowered into the drain on a rope to see if there were any further items relating to the kidnap to be found.

Almost as soon as he'd made it to the bottom of the shaft, Maskery found two more items which were of great interest to the investigation. Playing his torch over the scene, he spotted a handheld dymotape machine and a piece of sticking plaster cut to a size which could fit over a mouth. He also realised there was a labyrinth of tunnels running away in every direction which would afford a variety of unseen escape routes for the Black Panther after he'd taken possession of the ransom money.

Even if Ronald had been able to make the drop and the police successfully positioned themselves to apprehend the kidnapper, it soon became quite clear that they would have had no chance of catching him. In the darkness and confusion which always surrounds unfolding situations, while the police were laying in wait for someone to collect the ransom money, or indeed emerge from the drain. The Black Panther would have surfaced many hundreds of yards from the scene and well away from any containment operation. He'd have made good his escape and been long gone before those watching even began to have any inkling that they'd been fooled.

When he returned to the surface, Det Con Maskery was instructed to inspect an area of raised ground, hidden in a thicket of trees, where a leather jacket and a pair of binoculars had just been found. He uncovered another shaft which he was told to search. Unlike the raised land drain cover, entrance to this particular shaft was gained via a more traditional manhole type hinged cover.

Also, again unlike the main land drain, this one could be accessed by means of a metal ladder which ran in sections between several staging platforms. Carefully picking his way down, Maskery soon began to unearth more items which were left strewn on some of the platforms.

It was a dark and foreboding place. The cold and damp seemed to penetrate Maskery's clothes. He could hear noises which, at first he couldn't understand. Aside from the sound of running water emanating from the very bottom of the shaft, where it met one of the overflow systems, there was the un-nerving scuttle and squeak of rats. Despite its power, his torch couldn't fully pierce the blackness below so Maskery had no idea what he was descending into.

He'd penetrated some sixty feet into the shaft when he came across the last platform. He noticed some foam, similar to the material found in furniture, across which was a length of metal wire which had been secured to the side of the ladder by way of nut and bolt fastenings. On the platform itself, Maskery saw a sleeping bag laid out and contained within a clear plastic bag. There was also a tape recorder of the same make and model as the one found in the car.

The detective noticed that the wire was taut and disappeared into the darkness beneath the platform. Stepping down the last few rungs, he knelt on the platform, using his torch to illuminate the scene below, he got his head over the edge of the platform and peered into the gloom. There, almost face to face with him, was Lesley's body. She was naked and hanging by the neck from the other end of the wire.

A Post mortem on Lesley's body was conducted soon afterwards and the pathologist, Dr John

Brown reported that, even though her body had been found hanging, Lesley had not died from strangulation but a condition called vagal inhibition. In layman's terms, the shock the fall from the platform had caused her heart to stop beating. This was induced by the tight wire noose which triggered an alarm to her brain via the vagus nerve. Her brain responded to the nerve warning to reduce blood pressure by slowing down her heart. Because of the ligature, the response to the vagus nerve failed and Lesley's heart stopped beating altogether.

Dr Brown also recorded that Lesley was severely emaciated; in fact she weighed only seven stones (98lb) when discovered. Both her stomach and intestines were completely empty and he calculated that she had neither drunk nor eaten for several days before her death.

***

The recovery of Lesley's body was a delicate task, carried out carefully to not only afford the poor girl some measure of dignity, but to preserve what was now a crime scene. Even as she was being brought to the surface, news of the discovery had broken and a huge press pack gathered to witness the latest developments.

With Lesley's body removed, detectives went to the bottom of the shaft to hunt for further clues. Scattered about amongst other items was a length of discarded sticking plaster (which tests later revealed to have been used as a blindfold), a pair of size seven trainers, a roll of dymotape, a reporters notepad, a cassette tape, a pair of corduroy trousers, a Thermos flask, some electrical cable and a microphone. Everything the police recovered was carefully bagged up and sent off for forensic examination.

***

At a hastily convened press conference where the media was briefed on the discovery of Lesley's body, Det Ch Supt Booth made the following statement:
"How evil, how ruthless, how terribly wicked is this man that we've hunted for seven weeks. God above, I never dreamt in my wildest dreams that he'd do such a thing to a girl. It's terrible."

The kidnap had now become a murder inquiry and, as the crime had been committed within the precincts of the Staffordshire Police area, they took over the investigation. As a result Det Ch Supt Booth found himself effectively sidelined from the operation to catch the Black Panther.

Booth was determined to make sure he was not shut out of the investigation entirely. After all, West Mercia was the force who had taken the lead up until that point. The strained relations between senior officers of the police forces who were directly involved in the Lesley Whittle kidnapping case began to publicly surface. Detective Chief Superintendent Booth issued a statement to the press in which he said:

"We (West Mercia Police) want the Murderer. I don't care where he's arrested or by who he's arrested, we'll cooperate with anybody, but the hunt for that man is from here. These people (WM CID) have been working since November, since he came down to Langley and shot somebody. They've been working after that since he shot Mister Smith (Gerald Smith) and I've been working non-stop with them for nearly twenty-four hours every day for seven weeks and we'll work until we get him, and if we don't get him today we'll get him tomorrow."

Given the scale of the task and the publicity it was generating. The Chief Constable of Staffordshire decided to call in Scotland Yard to lead the murder hunt in an attempt to stem the near panic which was now sweeping the country.

Seven: Dragnet, Robberies & Arrest

Commander John Morrison was the head of Scotland Yard's Murder Squad

Morrison was a tough and resourceful officer who had earned a reputation as a detective the hard way – by solving crimes. He was born and raised on the Isle of Lewis, Scotland, and after leaving school aged fourteen, he worked on a fishing boat. He'd served with the Royal Navy during World War Two and thereafter joined the Metropolitan Police (after being rejected by Glasgow City Police for being too short) He eventually joined the CID where his performance on numerous serious cases ensured he rose through the ranks. Morrison's last high profile case was in 1973, when he'd been dispatched to Bermuda to investigate the murder of Sir Richard Sharples, the Governor of the island. He managed to track down the culprits who were later hanged for their crimes. This was the case which finally cemented his reputation as a manhunter who got results.

Commander Morrison had chosen Inspector Walter Boreham as his deputy for the investigation. Boreham was another well regarded detective who was known to get results. (Boreham went on to become the Chief Constable of the Ministry of Defence Police).

A major incident room was quickly established where Morrison and Boreham arrived to oversee events. His appointment was done in the glare of the media and from the off the Commander intended to utilise the power of the press to assist in this search for the Black Panther.

He was quick to make a statement in which he pointed out:

"This man is a cunning, vicious and sinister criminal and he is going to take a lot of catching. There is always the possibility that he will strike again. It is in everyone's interests that this man is brought to justice as soon as possible."

Although he'd been careful to make sure he left no fingerprints on any of the items he'd discarded in his getaway car or around Bathpool Park, Neilson didn't account for Commander Morrison issuing orders that every effort was to be made to track down where said items had been bought. The wily detective knew if he could pinpoint from where – for example – the tape recorders had been purchased, it was likely that he would be able to narrow his search down to a particular part of the country where the Black Panther lived, and perhaps even to a specific town or city. If real luck was on his side he might get a list of names and addresses relating to the manufacturers guarantees issued for said items.

Perhaps Neilson's biggest blunder was to leave the envelopes in the stolen car for, upon these, were examples of his handwriting. Morrison was quick to make a public appeal; with photographs of the envelopes being published across the press in the hope that someone may recognise it.

Commander Morrison was determined to build up a head of steam in the hunt for the Black Panther and thereafter keep the pressure on him all the way to his arrest. Details and photographs of the tape recorders and the torches, as well as other items were also fed to the media in the knowledge that they'd be splashed across TV screens and newspapers. Did anyone recognise the items? Had they sold them? Did they know anyone who owned them but no longer were in their possession? If anyone had any information regarding any of the items – however inconsequential they may feel it might be – they were encouraged to call the police.

The biggest mistake was one that Neilson had no idea he'd made. On one of the pages in the notebook which had been found at the bottom of the shaft where Lesley had been held captive, there was a single fingerprint. Forensics told Morrison that it matched those found on the spent cartridge cases. Calls were made to police forces across the UK in an attempt to match the print with those on their own records.

Commander Morrison also took the decision to call upon those forces who had already been investigating the post office robberies and murders committed by the Black Panther and requested they send duplicates of all their files on the case. Somewhere, among the thousands of pages of pages of witness statements or reports, there may just be a clue; a clue which on its own would mean nothing, but when pooled with others could crack the case. As one senior detective opined:

"We have his height, his build, his hair colour and his clothing. We knew everything about him except his name and address.

The hunt for the Black Panther consumed vast police resources across several forces where the wanted man had committed his various crimes, with several hundred officers dedicated to the task of finding him at any one time. In those days, the use of computers to aid police investigations was still very much in its infancy.

Today police can access records from the Police National Computer (PNC) database in a matter of seconds whereas, in the mid-1970s, everything was filed away in card index systems which were laborious to search through and subject to human error. One misplaced card, put in the wrong area by a force Criminal Records Office worker, would result in that file being overlooked during subsequent searches. This was serious enough when dealing with routine crimes, but in a case as serious as the hunt for the Black Panther, such an error could make the different between success and failure. Commander Morrison's team soon amassed in excess of eight million cards, each containing various snippets of information from forces across the North and the Midlands which had to be kept meticulously if they were to be of use to those hunting the Black Panther.

In an unprecedented move, and in an attempt to widen the search as far as possible, every police officer throughout the UK was issued with a card which read:

THE MURDER OF LESLEY WHITTLE

The following described man is wanted for this offence:

Description: 5'5" to 7", athletic build, possibly 35 years old, perhaps a young 40. Indication of size 7 footwear but not positive. Hair described generally as dark, no sideburns, trend inclined more to short back and sides, on occasion may be greased. Indication perhaps curly at ends.

Features of Face: Wild or staring eyes. Fresh complexion. Semi lantern jaw. Accent attributed to the Tipton Wednesbury side of Dudley, but may be assumed.

Enquiries have shown that this man has travelled over a wide area including Harrogate, Accrington, Langley West Midlands, Highley, Salop and Kidsgrove Staffordshire. He may also have connections with Redditch, Nottingham or Sutton Coldfield

The card went on to warn that the suspect would most likely be armed with a concealed .22 pistol which he would not hesitate to use if confronted. Interestingly, the point about Neilson's accent deflected from his real Yorkshire one, which was distinctly different to anything found in the areas described.

The investigation was relentless, during the next nine months the police had 600 men working 12 hours a day. More than 250,000 people were interviewed, 60,000 statements recorded and 40,000 questionnaires relating to the kidnap and the Black Panther's other crimes filled in.

Despite the best efforts of Commander Morrison and his team, and indeed dedicated squads across other force areas, the trail began to go cold. None of Morrison's appeals had yielded the hoped for results and the fingerprint came back as a negative match from every UK police force.

It seemed like the elusive Black Panther was going to slip the net once again.

The post Office offered a reward of £25,000 (approximately £232,000 - $342,500 in 2022 values) for information leading to the arrest and conviction of the Black Panther and wanted posters were prominently displayed across all their premises.

***

Neilson had been studying events as they unfolded from his attic planning room. He trawled through every newspaper in an attempt to keep up with developments. As the weeks passed he became more confident that the police were no nearer catching him than they had at the start of the kidnap.

Neilson found himself in a quandary. He knew that if he went to ground permanently and did nothing which may draw attention to himself, there was every chance that he'd never be caught. However, the time he'd spent executing Lesley's kidnap and the slim pickings he'd had before, during his last few robberies, meant he was now virtually broke. He'd fallen for Detective Chief Superintendent Booth's stunt with the TV news crew and was still kicking himself over what he thought to be his missed opportunity to collect the ransom money from Ronald Whittle at Bathpool Park. Hindsight and news reports made him realise that the 'unmarked' car and police panda car he'd seen in the car park as he lay in wait for Ronald's arrival were there innocently, and had no connection to the ransom drop. Had he held his nerve, he believed, he now would be £50,000 richer.

Neilson pondered over his options. He needed money – and fast. Plotting another kidnap would take much time and effort, time he didn't have. He considered himself to have been extremely lucky to evade the police during the kidnap of Lesley Whittle so he must find another way of generating large amounts of money in as short a space of time as possible. It didn't take him long to decide to return to doing what he considered he did best; robbing sub-post offices, and he set to work preparing for his next job.

***

Over the coming months several more robberies took place at sub-post offices across Yorkshire and the North Midlands. Police knew that they were the work of the Black Panther but, infuriatingly, he was still managing to stay one step ahead of every effort to catch him.

Media interest in the case had not waned and this put extra pressure on the police forces involved to come up with results. A watch was being kept on all new fingerprints entering the police system in the hope that the wanted man may just have found himself arrested for some unconnected misdemeanour.

It had been seven months since Commander Morrison had taken up the case and the Black Panther was still beyond his reach. Secretly, and among many other lines of inquiry, his team had been following up suggestions that the Black Panther was a Post Office employee. In those days the telephone network was owned by the Post Office and the Black Panther's apparent knowledge of how to evade telephone tracing during the Lesley Whittle kidnap prompted some to suspect he had inside knowledge. For obvious reasons, the police investigation drew another blank.

Meanwhile, braced for even more robberies and the possibility of yet another shooting, The Post Office itself issued written instructions to all Sub-post office staff in which they were advised to be on the lookout for suspicious activity, people or vehicles and report anything which gave them cause for concern to the police.

The police themselves had taken to paying particular attention to sub-post offices. While on night-time foot patrol or riding in panda cars, officers were ordered to check premises and remain on the alert in the vicinity of sub-post offices. It was hoped that, perhaps, a visible increase in police activity in and around these premises may help to ward off the Black Panther.

***

On the evening of December 11th 1975 in Mansfield, Nottinghamshire, a police panda car was plying its trade through the town. Inside were Police Constable's Stuart MacKenzie and Tony Wight. The pair were on the lookout for the usual instances of wrongdoing and eventually parked on Stainforth Street to observe passing traffic. In between looking out for drivers who were breaking the rules of the road, the pair busied themselves updating their pocket books.

The officers hadn't been there long when they happened to spot a man scurrying along on the pavement on the street opposite where they were parked. As soon as he noticed the panda car the man appeared to do his best to avert his gaze from the officers inside. It was dark and the scene was only lit with street lamps, so PCs Smith and Mackenzie couldn't see well enough to form a detailed impression of the figure, however, the way he appeared to be avoiding eye contact immediately alerted both their policeman's instincts, neither had it escaped their notice that they were quite close to the local sub-post office. They were both aware of the need to be on the lookout for suspicious activity within the vicinity of post offices so decided to stop and question the man.

"He's been up to something or is going to get up to something. Let's check him." PC MacKenzie said from the driver's seat as he turned the ignition key. At this point in time both officers were expecting nothing more than a routine stop, they'd have a brief chat with the man before – probably – sending him on his way.

They quickly caught up with the man, stopping just ahead thus giving PC Wight enough time to wind the front passenger window down. As the man drew level, PC Wight said.

"Good evening sir. At this time of night we like to check strangers out. Would you mind telling us where you've been?"

"I'm just going home from work." The man replied.

When asked his name and address the man said he was John Moxton of Chapel-en-le-Frith.

PC MacKenzie had his pocketbook out and was writing down what was being said during the exchange. The next words he heard were.

"Don't Move! Any tricks and you're dead!"

He looked up to see the man holding a sawn-off shotgun which he was pointing at the pair through the open window.

"F*****G Hell!" Exclaimed PC MacKenzie.

"Jesus Christ! Not in Woodhouse!" Were the first words uttered by PC Wight.

The man had them both covered and it was obvious from his demeanour that he meant business.

"You!" He barked at PC Wight. "In the back!"

PC Wight was forced to clamber over the passenger seat into the rear of the car where the man ordered him to sit hard against the corner, directly behind the driver's seat where he could be kept an eye on. Seemingly satisfied that both officers weren't going to resist, the man climbed in beside PC MacKenzie then pushed the barrels of his gun hard under the policeman's armpit. After warning them both not to look at him he growled:

"Drive!"

"Where to?"

"Just drive!"

PC MacKenzie set off slowly, not wanting to spook the gunman into squeezing the trigger. His fears were confirmed when, a few seconds later, the man said.

"Drive normally or you'll both be dead!"

In the back seat, PC Wight knew he was under observation and, even in the gunman's peripheral vision, and move he made would be seen and result in his colleague being killed before he could even get to grips with the man.

Up front, PC MacKenzie had made eye contact with PC Wight in the rear view mirror, and was attempting to signal for him to surprise then disarm the gunman. PC Wight was in no position to do anything at that particular point in time; it was best, he concluded, to bide his time until an opportunity arose where he could act.

As the panda car drove along Southwell Road, it approached a fork in the road. PC MacKenzie asked which way he should go and the gunman said 'towards Blidworth'. The fact that he'd pronounced Blidworth 'Blidorth' convinced both officers that they were dealing with a local.

PC MacKenzie suddenly feared that the gunman wanted to take them to Blidworth woods (which is situated close to the famous Sherwood Forest of Robin Hood fame) where he would kill them both before making good his escape. If he was to prevent this from happening he would have to take immediate action.

Without warning, in one fluid move, PC MacKenzie swung the steering wheel from side to side, slammed on the brakes and pushed himself into his seat to dislodge the gun from his armpit. The sudden violence of the manoeuvre took the gunman by surprise and presented PC Wight with the window of opportunity he'd been waiting for. In a split second, before the man could react, PC Wight had hold of the gun, pushing it up and away from his friend. There was an almighty bang as the shotgun was discharged up into the roof, missing PC Mackenzie's head by a matter of only a few inches.

In the same instant, with the car now stationary, PC MacKenzie threw himself out of the door and rolled onto the tarmac. Inside the panda car, a violent struggle had already developed. Seeing his colleague tumble out of the car convinced PC Wight that he'd been caught in the gun blast and either seriously injured or killed.

PC Wight had managed to get the gun away from the man and had one arm around his neck, pulling him so hard that his opponent was half dragged over the seat.

Meanwhile, in the confusion of it all, PC MacKenzie thought his friend had been shot. He jumped to his feet and ran around the car to the passenger door where he intended to get to grips with the gunman.

In the confines of the car, the gunman was putting up a tremendous struggle. PC Wight elbowed him hard in the face twice in an attempt to subdue him but to no effect. The man was very strong and fighting like a wildcat.

By now, PC MacKenzie was in position and could see the fight in the car. Swinging open the passenger door, he grabbed the man and dragged him onto the pavement where the pair began to wrestle furiously. PC Wight clambered out of the car to join in the fight. By this time both officers saw that the man was reaching for something inside his coat. His strength meant that both PCs were barely able to contain him but, somehow, they managed to stop him from doing what he was trying to do.

The drama was being played out in front of a local fish & chip shop. Roy Morris was a coal miner at a nearby pit. He'd been out for the evening at the local working men's club and decided to leave early then call into the shop for some supper. He'd seen the panda car skidding to a halt followed by a loud bang (which Mister Morris didn't recognise as a gunshot). As the chip shop customers looked on, they saw PC MacKenzie getting to grips with a man. With no further hesitation, Mr. Morris and a few others ran out of the shop.

"What's going off?!" Mister Morris shouted as PCs MacKenzie and Wight were struggling to keep the man from breaking away.

"Hold his hands!" PC MacKenzie replied.

Now there is no doubt that Neilson was strong, so strong that two fit young police officers – who themselves were used to physical confrontation – were having great difficulty in restraining him, but Mister Morris worked in the mines, hewing coal eight hours a day. As a result, the gunman may have been strong, but he was no match for him.

Mister Morris had hold of the man's forearms and, in one move, had them together behind his back. Immediately, PC MacKenzie had his handcuffs out and placed on the man's wrists.

While he continued to put up a violent struggle as he attempted to break free of the police, the people from the chip shop (who had now been joined by others who'd been standing at a nearby bus stop) overpowered him. The man was pulled to his feet and dragged to some metal railings where PC Wight used his cuffs to secure him to them. Even though he'd been well and truly restrained, the man kept struggling in a futile attempt to break out of the handcuffs.

It's the author's opinion that, had it not been for the timely intervention of Mister Morris, the mysterious gunman may well have been able to break away from the officers and, perhaps, even make good his escape.

Both officers were dishevelled and exhausted from their labours and, while his colleague called the incident in on his radio, PC Wight conducted a body search of the gunman. Chillingly, on his left hip, was a large hunting knife. This was the weapon the man had been reaching for. Under his coat, was a shotgun cartridge bandolier containing twenty-two 12 bore rounds. Tucked into his left boot was another, smaller, sheath knife. He'd also been carrying a small canvas holdall type bag which, when searched, was found to contain a brace and bit, gloves and a face mask of the type as described by previous Black Panther victims.

Unwittingly, for at that point in time they still had no inkling who they'd arrested, PCs MacKenzie and Wright had ended the reign of the Black Panther.

***

Even before he arrived in custody, questions were already being asked about the mystery gunman.

He'd identified himself as John Moxton of Chapel-en-le-Frith, and checks revealed there was no such person residing in that area. As soon as he'd been arrested he'd fallen silent, refusing to speak to anyone. He also resisted attempts to take his fingerprints which meant he couldn't be identified for who he really was.

When news of the incident reached senior CID

officers they immediately began to wonder if the two PCs had actually caught the notorious Black Panther? Crucial points regarding the description matched so, soon, they were confident enough to make their suspicions known to the murder team in Staffordshire.

'We think we've got your man' was the telex received in the major incident room in Staffordshire. As a detailed description of both the incident and the gunman was made available, Commander Morrison was alerted. A telephone call with the head of Nottinghamshire CID was enough to convince Morrison that they were indeed onto on to something and he was driven to Mansfield Police Station to interview the suspect himself.

Neilson was proving as elusive in custody as he had been while at large. He was still being uncooperative and maintaining his bogus identity. The only thing the police managed to get from him were a couple of mugshots which, by virtue of the fact that he'd been elbowed in the face by PC Wight during their fight and later 'roughed up' a little by bystanders as they helped to subdue him while he was being handcuffed to the railings, were of little use. He looked like he'd gone five rounds with Henry Cooper so the resulting photograph couldn't be matched to existing records as it was distributed across the country. Even had he been unscathed, Neilson's image would not have raised any flags as he was unknown to the police anyway.

The only thing the police had to go on was the fact that the gunman wasn't wearing gloves when he'd been arrested. Could a forensic examination of the items found on him, or indeed the places where he'd been in contact with the panda car, yield a result?

When Commander Morrison arrived to interview the mystery gunman he – Neilson – was still saying nothing. Perhaps harking back to his military days, he was sticking to his own variation of the 'name, rank and number' mantra. Despite not being able to provide an address and being told there was no John Moxton of Chapel-en-le-Frith (though, all the police had to go on at that time was the electoral roll; a list of residents who were eligible to vote. The electoral roll could not be relied upon to give a truly accurate picture of the population, as it was entirely possible that 'John Moxton' had moved into the area after the last list was compiled). Checks with other agencies also drew a blank.

With the suspect saying nothing to him when they first sat down in the interview room, Commander Morrison decided to put himself on the front foot by issuing 'John Moxton's' mugshot to the media. Even in his battered state, a friend or family member was sure to instantly recognise the face and call the major incident room with a name and address. Commander Morrison put his plan to 'Moxton' in the hope that it might shake him into revealing his true identity but, to his surprise, the suspect refused to budge.

By this time, and before the photograph was circulated to the media, a report had been received from the forensics people. Although all the items found on the gunman had been handled by others during the chaos surrounding his arrest, their prints had been quickly eliminated. Several partial fingerprints remained which were intact enough to be lifted and examined. These were positively identified as matching those found on the .22 cartridge cases left behind during previous Black Panther shootings and, crucially, the notepad found at the scene of Lesley Whittle's incarceration.

At another interview, when Commander Morrison put it to the suspect that prints recovered from his shotgun matched those on evidence found at the scene of the Lesley Whittle kidnapping and other Black Panther crimes, he was shocked when the man suddenly began to talk. His name, he said, wasn't John Moxton, but Donald Neilson. He gave his home address in Bradford and, looking Morrison straight in the eye, confessed that, yes, he was the Black Panther.

By this time, news had begun to leak about the possible capture of the Black Panther and the press and TV news crews started to assemble outside where Neilson was being held in the hope of landing a scoop.

Detectives arrived at Neilson's Bradford home to begin a detailed search of the property. Upstairs, in the loft, and after gaining forcible entry through the locked hatch, they entered the Black Panther's secret planning room. The place was a veritable treasure trove of evidence. They uncovered another sawn-off shotgun, bandoliers containing 12 bore cartridges, several boxes of 12 bore cartridges, .22 long rifle ammunition, a .22 rimfire pistol (the one used in his murders), a rifle, a dymotape machine and rolls of dymotape, hoods, combat style clothing, housebreaking tools, two crossbows, telescopic sights, gloves, wire (of the same type used for Lesley Whittle's noose), knives and other incriminating items. Chillingly, and in a narcissistic celebration of his alter ego, Neilson also had a statue of a black panther prominently displayed on a ledge in the attic.

The find was communicated to Commander Morrison, who set about preparing another interview with Neilson. He planned to hit the suspect with photographs and documentary proof of the items found at his home and how they related to the Black Panther's exploits in an attempt to make Neilson fully confess to his crimes.

As they sat down for their interview, Commandeer Morrison knew that the evidence he had against Neilson was already overwhelming. A full and frank confession would simply be the icing on the cake.

As Morrison suspected – when he was shown the photographs taken in his attic room and was given details of the forensic evidence the police had which directly tied him to both the kidnap and death of Lesley Whittle, the shooting of Gerald Smith and the murders of Donald Skepper, Derek Astin and Sidney Grayland – Neilson realised there was no way out. Instead of trying in vain to refute the evidence, he went into damage limitation mode.

"I want to tell you the truth," Proclaimed Neilson. "I hate all these lies. I want people to know the truth. I will not tell you lies like the newspapers."

In all, the interview lasted some nine hours. This marathon session saw Commander Morrison run through each detail of every single one of Neilson's crimes. The biggest bone of contention between the two men centred around the fate of Lesley Whittle.

"I didn't murder her." He insisted when pressed by Morrison. He went on to claim that he didn't know who he was going to take from the Whittle residence, and just happened to enter Lesley's room by chance.

After he'd concluded the interview, Commander Morrison knew he had everything he needed in terms of verbal accounts to make sure the charges he was going to lay at Neilson's feet would stick. When all the physical evidence was added into the mix, the Black Panther's prospects of evading guilty verdicts on each and every count were virtually impossible.

Donald Neilson was formally charged with numerous offences which ranged from murder, kidnap, stealing firearms, possession of firearms, He was also charged with the attempted murders of PC MacKenzie and Margaret Grayland.
The list of charges was long and the case against him complex. Given the weight of evidence against him, Neilson backtracked a little, refusing to acknowledge his guilt.

He was remanded in custody until he could be brought to trial.

Eight: Trial, Prison & Other Events

The Trial of Donald Neilson began on the 14th June 1976 at Oxford Crown Court. Given the nature of case, it had been decided to try him on two separate occasions. This first trial was to focus on the kidnap and murder of Lesley Whittle. Despite the overwhelming evidence to the contrary, he pleaded not guilty.

The summer of 1976 will be remembered by many as the great heatwave, in fact, such were the temperatures inside the courtroom that the QC's and the judge forewent the wearing of the traditional wigs. Outside, great queues of onlookers gathered, each one attempting to catch a glimpse of the infamous Black Panther as he was brought in and out of court. The courtroom itself was packed with press and the public all eager to watch events as they unfolded.

Neilson was defended by Gilbert Gray QC. As for the kidnap itself, there was nothing to base a defence upon so Mister Gray concentrated upon the murder charge. He contended that Lesley Whittle had not been pushed to her death by his client, but instead had accidentally fallen from the ledge and died as a result. He was keen to stress that over the period of her incarceration, while Neilson was attempting to have the ransom money delivered, he had not only left her a flask of hot chicken soup, but had subsequently fed her with spaghetti and meatballs, and bought fish and chips which he took down the shaft to Lesley. Mister Gray also pointed out that Neilson had provided his victim with a sleeping bag which was designed for use in cold weather environments as well as a piece of foam to act as a mattress of sorts. In addition, he'd provided Lesley with a bottle of brandy, six paperback books, a copy of the Times and two magazines, a puzzle game plus a torch and spare batteries. The items as listed by Mister Gray were all recovered by police in the shaft and, he argued, were clear proof that Neilson had every intention of keeping his victim alive.

The prosecution contested each one of Mister Gray's claims, saying instead that Neilson had returned to the shaft after the failed Bathpool Park ransom drop and, believing that he'd been 'betrayed', in a fit of rage he'd pushed Lesley to her death. It was also explained that, since his arrest, Neilson had not displayed any remorse over the kidnap or the death of Lesley.

In an attempt to have the murder charge quashed, Mister Gray had played his only hand but lost. Two weeks after the trial began, it ended with a unanimous guilty verdict on both counts.

The sentence handed down was life imprisonment

On the 6th of July, Neilson found himself back in court to face the other charges. Unfortunately for the family of Gerald Smith, Neilson was to evade a murder charge. Gerald had finally succumbed to the wounds inflicted upon him by Neilson, but had died outside the parameters where a murder charge could be brought. *In those days anyone dying more than one year and a day after an attack from wounds sustained during said attack were not deemed to have been murdered. (Directly as a result of the Black Panther case, the law was changed).*

The prosecution case and physical evidence against Neilson was overwhelming and it can be seen as a testament to the dexterity of his defence council that the attempted murder charges against Mrs Grayland and PC MacKenzie were downgraded to grievous bodily harm and possession of a shotgun with intent to endanger life respectively.

It came as no surprise to anyone when, after a three week trial, the jury found Neilson guilty.

Neilson's counsel, Mister Gilbert Gray QC, made one final impassioned plea in an attempt to persuade the judge not to 'snuff out' the only light left in Mr Neilson's life – the hope that he might eventually be released. Mister Gray said 'Neilson knew he had to face very long, dark days of imprisonment, But he needed some little hope to assure his sanity.'

Mister Gray also went on to say that he thought there was a desire from the public to see the words once spoken by Mr Neilson come true; 'that if the police thought he was the Black Panther they would throw away the key'.

The judge, Justice Mars-Jones interrupted him:

"I am not surprised he said that. He shot down three sub-postmasters who had a duty to protect public money, large amounts of money. They were doing just that when he shot them."

In a hushed courtroom, Mister Mars-Jones, delivered his summing up. Neilson stood and listened, showing no emotion whatsoever as the judge explained that the enormity of his crimes put him in a class apart from almost all convicted murderers in recent years. He went on to say that the evidence against Neilson had been overwhelming. He has struck terror into the hearts of postmasters, sub-postmasters, and their families throughout the county.

"You were never without a loaded shotgun or other loaded weapons when you went on your criminal expeditions and never hesitated to shoot to kill when you were in danger of arrest or detection. You showed no mercy whatsoever."

The judge also referred to the kidnapping of Lesley Whittle as the ultimate in villainy, yet another of Neilson's 'enterprise that ended in murder.'

Mr Justice Mars-Jones then delivered his coup de grâce, handing Neilson Five life sentences, to run concurrently with the one he'd been sentenced to for the murder and kidnap of

Lesley Whittle. *One of the life sentences was given for his attack on Margaret Grayland.*

Neilson showed no emotion as sentence was passed on him. He simply swallowed hard and lowered his head.

Neilson then raised his head to look directly at the judge as Mr Mars-Jones said that, 'in his judgement, such was the gravity and enormity of offences committed by him that life in his case would mean life.'

The trial ended when the judge said "Take him down," and Neilson turned and was led away into the cells by two burly police officers.

After the conviction but prior to his sentencing, Mister Mars-Jones had studied a report on Neilson which had been conducted by Dr Lionel Haward, a consultant psychologist at the University of Surrey. Dr Hayward said he found Neilson to be a man of high intelligence, about twenty per cent above average. The report also pointed out that Neilson was suffering from a psycho-pathological condition of some severity, but one that was not sufficient to diminish responsibility on his part.

Neilson had, Dr Hayward said, a complex personality, showed signs of extreme rigidity and inflexibility, and was obsessive to an extremely high degree, especially when it came to detailed planning.

The report ended with the following: 'He was not a man who desired violence, but because of his inability to cope with defeat in situations where his plans failed, his intelligence broke down.'

***

Neilson was taken from court under armed guard to a maximum security prison. He'd already been categorised as highly dangerous whilst on remand, so was placed under the strictest security arrangements the prison system had to offer. Such was his reputation as a dangerous individual that he was kept in isolation, well away from the general prison population.

After the case, Neilson's solicitor, Barrington Black, announced that an appeal had been lodged against the verdict in the Lesley Whittle case and that an appeal involving the post office murders was being considered.
In the event, nothing came of any of it, with the appeals being dismissed.

***

The Story didn't end there. According to reports at the time, when Neilson failed to return home after his arrest by PCs MacKenzie and

Wight in Mansfield, his wife, Irene, started to get worried and burned around fifty postal orders in their coal fire of their lounge. The remains of the postal orders were spotted by detectives as they searched the property. As a result, Irene was charged with cashing more than eighty stolen postal orders which had been taken in one Neilson's post office raids.

At court she claimed to have been forced into cashing the postal orders in various post offices across the West Riding. The solicitor acting on her behalf solicitor, Barrington Black (who had represented her husband), placed the blame on Donald Neilson, claiming that he – Neilson – exercised complete control over his wife, with the result that Irene was afraid to defy him. Mister Black said that Neilson was a "Svengali, who had exercised a hypnotic influence over Irene." And. "He was a quasi-military figure who barked orders at his wife and daughter and woe betide anyone who disobeyed him."

Mister Black impressed upon the court that this portrayal of Neilson was accurate and made during the course of several visits to Donald Neilson in prison.

In the event, Irene was found guilty. Under any other circumstances, it was almost a foregone conclusion that, if convicted, Irene would not be handed a custodial sentence; after all, she was of previous good character and had never been in trouble with the police, however, a court report made to the presiding magistrates contradicted his assessment regarding the direction the court's award should take.

Black asked the magistrates if Irene really deserved to be harshly treated for a situation that he continue to argue was forced upon her. He stressed that last three years she'd spent with Neilson before his arrest had been "hell".

Mister Black's impassioned pleas fell on deaf ears. While passing sentence, the magistrates said that 'while they had every sympathy with a lady before the courts for the first time, they regarded her activities as a deliberate course of conduct.' Irene was handed a twelve months prison sentence.

An appeal was immediately lodged and
Gilbert Gray QC (the barrister who had defended Neilson) was appointed to represent her.

At the subsequent court hearing Mister Gray produced Donald Neilson as a surprise witness. Mister Gray explained that he 'was anxious that the court should be aware of the pressure and constraints placed upon Mrs Neilson as a result of her husband.' As part of his summation, Mister Gray explained that Neilson 'was the man who struck fear and dread into pretty much the whole community and this woman lived with him'.

Despite Mister Gray's spirited imploration, the judges found Donald Neilson's testimony to have a 'vagueness' and nothing presented was of sufficient substance to make a difference. As a result they upheld the court's decision regarding Irene's conviction and sentence.

While Irene was in prison, she was approached by a leading UK newspaper and subsequently paid a large amount for the Neilson's story which then ran in serialised form.

Irene served eight months in prison before being released for good behaviour.

***

Donald Neilson spent the next thirty-three years in prison before being diagnosed with motor neurone disease (a muscle wasting condition) in 2009. Throughout his time in prison he had remained on the category A list. He'd been confined in the most secure prisons across the UK, being moved at regular intervals for security purposes and had spent his time confined to his cell.

After he'd been diagnosed with motor neurone disease, medical reports confirmed the severity of his condition was such that he should be moved from Full Sutton maximum security prison in East Yorkshire, to Norwich Prison, Norfolk, where his condition could be better attended to. Norwich Prison has a specialist medical wing where complex and challenging needs can be given far better care than within the normal prison system. By this time Neilson's condition was becoming increasingly worse and soon reached the point where he was depended on others to carry out the most menial of everyday tasks. That said, such was the authorities view of Neilson that, even as he lay helpless and dying, prison officers were assigned to maintain a constant 'bed watch' on him.

Donald Neilson died on 18th December 2011. A statement released later stated:
"He (Neilson) was a challenging and uncooperative patient and staff at the prison are to be commended for the level of care they provided which was equitable with that he would have received in the community."

The coroner recorded that he'd died of natural causes, after finally succumbing to a bout of pneumonia.

***

So ended a dark chapter in British criminal history. Neilson died a lonely man. His family didn't visit him. Over the years he will have pondered on the many 'what ifs' but it's doubtful that he expended much time and effort thinking of the horror he visited upon the victims of his crimes.

Nine: Further Reading

Other books in the 'True Crime' series.

The Krays: Their Life And Crimes

They came from the tough streets of London's east-end. They grew up together, they fought together, they ruled vast swathes of the city together, they murdered together, and together everyone considered them unstoppable. Ronnie and Reggie Kray's reputation for violence preceded them wherever they went and was instrumental in propelling them to a notoriety which has never been equalled, before or since, throughout the brutal history of British organised crime.

Presented concisely, yet packed with detail, this book concentrates on telling the true story of the Krays, their rise to the top of London's criminal underworld, their subsequent murderous exploits and how they were finally brought to justice.

In recounting the rise and fall of London's most notorious mobsters, Dan Shaw leads the reader into the very heart of post war London gangland. It wasn't a place for the timid. Dare you enter violent world of The Krays? 'The Krays' is the first instalment in the 'True Crime' series by Dan Shaw.

The Great Train Robbery

In the early hours of Thursday 8th August 1963 at rural Cheddington in Buckinghamshire, a Travelling Post

Office train was on the final leg of its journey from Glasgow to London. Complying with a red signal light, the train was brought to a stop on a remote section of track. Suddenly, and without warning, the engine was boarded and taken over by masked men. So began legend of the 'Great Train Robbery'....
Dan Shaw, author of 'The Krays: Their Life and Crimes' recounts the dramatic true story of that most audacious of crimes. Presented succinctly, from the start this book places the reader at the very heart of the action and gives them a bird's eye view of the roller coaster of a story which encompasses everything from genesis of the plan, its execution, the police hunt, capture and trial, subsequent escapes from prison and life on the run.
It's a real life high octane thriller which will have the reader on the edge of their seat.

The Great Train Robbery is the second in Dan Shaw's 'True Crime' series.

The Real Bank Job

It was the most audacious crime of the 1970's; a gang of villains tunnelled their way into the safety deposit box vault of Lloyds Bank on Baker Street, London. The 'walkie-talkie' robbery (as it became known) was later immortalised in the hit 2008 film 'The Bank Job' starring Jason Statham.

Dan Shaw, Author of 'The Krays: Their Life and Crimes' and 'The Great Train Robbery' presents the explosive true account of one of the most daring and ingenious heists in British criminal history. It's a story packed with suspense and intrigue, near misses, and edge of the seat plot twists.
Dan Shaw has managed to cram all the drama of the real bank job into one concise yet electrifying account, taking

the reader by the scruff of the neck and propelling them into the centre of what is a truly astounding story.

Dare you join the gang as they attempt the real 'Bank Job'?

These books are available from Amazon in both eBook and physical formats. They can also be ordered from some bookshops.

Please look out for more Dan Shaw 'True Crime' titles. They will appear over time.

Printed in Great Britain
by Amazon